Any Road Will Take You There

Also by David W. Berner

Accidental Lessons

After Opium: Stories

Knowing What to Steal

Any Road Will Take You There

A journey of fathers and sons

David W. Berner

Dream *of* Things
Downers Grove Illinois USA
dreamofthings.com

Any Road Will Take You There

Copyright © 2014 by David W. Berner

First Dream of Things edition, September 2014
Published by Dream of Things, Downers Grove, Illinois USA
dreamofthings.com

Dream of Things provides discounts to educators, book
clubs, writers groups, and others. Contact customerservice@
dreamofthings.com or call 847-321-1390.

Publisher's Cataloging-in-Publication data:
Berner, David W.
    Any road will take you there : a journey of fathers and sons
/ David W. Berner.
    p. cm.
    ISBN 9780988439092

1. Berner, David W. --Travel --United States. 2. Fathers and
sons. 3. Automobile travel --United States. 4. United States
--Description and travel. I. Title.

E169.Z82 B473 2014
E169.Z82 --dc23   2014950167
Book design: Susan Veach

For Casey and Graham

"Though we travel the world over to find the beautiful,
we must carry it within us or we will find it not."
– Ralph Waldo Emerson

Contents

Acknowledgements

Stories are never told alone, but rather emerge from the truths of many. That's why I have several people to thank. Casey and Graham are the inspired souls of this book. The story would not have been written without their input and spirit, and I am eternally grateful to them for allowing me to tell my version of this journey. Thanks to Marie, their mother, for supporting this wild idea from the beginning and encouraging me to get out on the road with the boys. And, thanks to Brad Holley, my great friend, for his unflinching enthusiasm for this idea. His energy helped fuel our trip. This book would have remained only a dream without the support of the Chicago Writers Association and especially The Kerouac Project of Orlando. I completed much of the writing while the Writer-in-Residence at the Kerouac House in Florida. The summer I lived and worked in Jack's home was a turning point in the development of this story. Many sincere thanks to Janet Rosen of Sheree Bykofsky Associates, Inc. Her belief in this book was resolute. Thanks to those who closely read, made suggestions, helped shape, or edit the words in the various forms of the manuscript—Lisa Mottola Hudon, Trude Holli, Rosalie White, Jackie Woods, Rick Kaempfer, David Stern, Randy Richardson, Mike Robinson, Scott Whitehair, Janna Marlies Maron, and Diane Berner. In addition, I must thank my mother, Gloria. She forever supported my writing and gave me the gift of a lifelong love of the written word. Finally, the deepest expression of gratitude goes to my father, Norm. His heart beats on every page of this book.

Chapter 1
Four Generations of Men

I was the teenager with the dog-eared paperback copy of Jack Kerouac's *On the Road* tucked in the back pocket of my Levi's. I can still see the cover: black with the title in white block letters below a small square of blue and orange rectangles, like pieces of a broken jigsaw puzzle. I'm sure the square was meant to represent modern art, a Picasso-esque painting. I found the edition in a used bookstore in Pittsburgh where I grew up, and I cherished it, held it tight to my chest. I so badly wanted to be Sal Paradise, the book's narrator, the character Kerouac based on himself, and to do nothing more than get in a car and hit the road.

Like Sal, I was a bit of a disillusioned young man. Not a sour, angst-laden kid, but certainly one shrouded with uncertainty. I wasn't alone. Like most of my friends, I wondered if I was good enough, smart enough, handsome enough, and fretted over what in the world I was going to do with my life. There were innocent dreams of being a musician, or at least spinning the records I loved on the radio as a disc jockey. I wrote songs and lyrics, and I honestly believed if I worked hard enough, I could write profound words like

Dylan, Neil Young, or Leonard Cohen. I played coffeehouses and a few campus bars, but I was only acting the part. I was no Bob Dylan. Not even close. But maybe, like Sal Paradise, I, too, could find inspiration. Paradise wanted to write, and I wanted to compose lyrics and music that I would be proud to play, proud to say were my compositions. But instead of actually going on the road to find insight, I just kept reading *On the Road,* writing in the margins and underlining passages, defaulting to what was on the pages instead of in the real bus stations, train yards, and on the highways. I was romanced by the book, but didn't have the necessary courage to live it. Still, there were sections that gave me shots of adrenaline and faith that I could somehow find my place in the world. Right from the beginning, Kerouac's words screamed out to me. At the end of the first chapter, he wrote about heading out on the road and finding girls and visions, believing this would help him find his way. Passages like that one throughout the novel gave me hope that I could someday put myself out there, allow the energy of life and experience to envelop me. And if I did, maybe life's jewels would come my way.

The book starts with a downer. A young Paradise is disillusioned and depressed about his break-up with his wife and his life as a struggling writer. But after a series of manic cross-country road trips with the character Dean Moriarty—an impulsive experience junkie from Denver who had spent some time in jail—Paradise finds joy and purpose. Sal figures it out by going on the road. But in those days, I didn't have the guts to act on the messages in Kerouac's road bible. Hell, I didn't even own a car. Plus, I was in school, had classes to attend, tuition to pay, reasons to be responsible. Despite this, *On the Road* made a weighty impression. Before Kerouac, I was an ambitious and calculated undergrad, planning out my future like a grocery list of things to accomplish. After Kerouac, I saw the possibilities in exploration, in experience, and the attraction of living life in the moment, honestly and authentically. Maybe I wasn't prepared to jump behind the wheel and hit the pavement, be a real road rebel, but I could certainly read Kerouac, learn from Sal and Dean, and be vicariously transformed. *On the Road* offered the story of discovery and the liberty to long for something more meaningful. This was the medicine that was Kerouac, an elixir for a young man's soul.

But it wasn't until years later when I was a middle-aged man that I was able to reach deep down and honestly consider putting a bit of Kerouac's manual of self-discovery into practice. It was the spark from an unexpected discovery; a surprising and eye-opening find that re-ignited Kerouac's spirit in me. Deep inside the middle drawer of a cabinet in my mother's living room, hidden from view for decades, was a photograph, one that had been kept from me for more than forty years.

It was a few years after my father's death, and I was helping my mother clean out decades of accumulated clothes, books, record albums, and old receipts from desks, closets, and chest-of-drawers. The old Kodak snapshot was among a stack of dozens of other faded and cracked photos stuffed inside a small shoebox. It was taken when I was five years old with a film camera, one technical progression prior to the Polaroid Instamatic. The setting is the family room of a relative's home in front of the fireplace. A plastic poinsettia ornament hangs on the wall in the photo's background, so it is Christmas. The photograph captures four generations of men—my great-grandfather, my grandfather, my father, and me. I look bewildered and uncertain. My father and grandfather smile awkwardly, the way people do when they are coaxed to grin for a camera. And the man in the middle with his arms folded across his chest, appears he wants it unmistakably known that he has no interest in being part of the picture at all. Considering the remarkable moment it recorded, the intersection of the lifetimes of fathers and sons, I was puzzled that it had not been framed and displayed in a place of prominence. When I asked my mother why, she unfolded a story that had been tucked away in that cabinet drawer for a generation.

When my father was in high school, his father left his mother. Walked out. But he didn't simply disappear, move to another town, or run off with his secretary as if he were a character in the clichéd tale of a man who finds himself in bed with the woman who navigates his phone messages and business calendar. Instead my grandfather moved into a house just down the street, another home in a quiet suburban neighborhood, so he could be with the woman he said he loved, the mother of my father's best friend. My dad would go to bed at night, staring at the ceiling, knowing his father was sleeping with a woman he often saw working in her garden, at the grocery store, or sitting in the pews at the Catholic church just a mile away. This was the woman who likely gave my father a bottle of Coke to cool off during a hot summer day when he and his friend, her son, had returned from an afternoon of delivering the daily newspaper to the homes on my dad's paper route. This was the woman who waved hello to my father when he'd walk home from school, when he'd ride his bike past her house on a Saturday morning. Now, he was doing everything he could to avoid her. If he saw her on the street, he undoubtedly ducked between the houses. If he saw her at church, he probably stood in the back by the confessional and left before she did. If she were sitting on her porch in an old wicker chair puffing her cigarettes, he would likely walk through the backyards to keep from her sight and steer clear of the peppery smell of what he thought were Parliaments, the same brand his mother smoked. Dad had to drop out of school to work as a carpenter on a homebuilder's crew to support his now fatherless family. He never again played high school football and lost the time he once had to paint and sketch. My father had been a talented artist. On the walls of his bedroom, he had created pencil drawings of marshes and lakes with ducks and loons flying above them. When his mother repainted the room she painted around the artwork, leaving the originals untouched. And in his dresser drawer, Dad kept dozens of charcoal sketches of Jackie Gleason, boxer Billy Conn, and Mickey Mouse. From what I'd been told, it was decades before my father ever again spoke to the neighbor woman, his best friend, or his father.

In the photo, Dad is the one on the far left smiling because the cameraman told him to. He does it convincingly, his dignity fueling the emotion on his face, masking harbored bitterness. Wearing a gray Bing Crosby-style cardigan and a red open-collared shirt underneath, Dad stands with his shoulders back and his head up, his eyes looking directly into the camera's lens.

David W. Berner

See, Father, I didn't leave MY son. I would never leave my son. I'm not like you. On the far right, alone in his own presence, stands my grandfather. He's the one smiling selfconsciously, the right corner of his mouth turned up, the left turned down in a contorted grin. His shoulders slump, his white dress shirt is crisp, his maroon tie taut against his collar, a tie clip pulling it tight against the shirt's center placket. In his shirt pocket rests a pair of glasses, habitually removed from his face when someone calls for a camera. His salt-and-pepper hair is combed straight back from his forehead, the way he had worn it for decades. And in the center of the photo, standing like a reluctant six-foot high barricade between my father and his, is my great-grandfather, the tallest in the photograph. His arms are crossed over his chest and his eyes look, not at the camera, but defiantly away from it. Turn-of-the-century wire rim glasses rest on his long, thin nose, his white hair is combed straight back like his son's, and his white pocket square peaks out *just right* from the chest pocket of his milk chocolate-colored suit coat, the same suit he wore when he played the piano at the silent movie house in town, taught weekly music lessons, and attended Sunday masses. A decades-old suit that still fit.

Whoever was on the other side of the lens unflinchingly coaxed these three men into standing together for this unlikely photograph. *This is a moment we may never see again. It's family history. Why don't you all get together for a picture? How wonderful.* Those on the other side of the camera were uninformed of the family backstory, or boldly ignored it. No matter, the reality was that none of the men had stood together like this before, physically or emotionally, and no matter the opportunity, the

6

holiday, or the history, the camera failed to disguise the layers of bitterness, shame, or contempt.

The fourth in the photo, standing directly in front of my great-grandfather, is a child. It's me. A little boy who has been pulled and pushed by the photographer into this implausible collage. *Come on. Get in there. Stand in the middle. That's it. Straighten your collar. Put your hands by your sides. That's your grandfather, you know? Your great-grandfather, too. How about that?* There were certainly many relatives around that day, enticing this group to pose together. It was the holiday season, a celebration of family. Those keenly aware of the discord may have believed it was time to forget the past and openly call for a truce, but I'm also confident there were others who knew nothing about what these men carried like anvils in their hearts. *No one is getting any younger. This may be the last time they'll ever be in the same room together. Anyone have a camera?* Or maybe it's simpler than that, more innocent. Maybe someone was merely thinking of me. *The grandchildren should have this photograph. There's something so special about having all these men together, fathers and sons. It will be something they'll cherish forever.*

Some fifteen years after the photo was taken, a phone call came to my parent's home. And, as was customarily the case at our house, my mother answered it.

"Gloria, this is Norman's old friend from high school."

It was my father's childhood companion, the teenage boy who grew up with my father's dad, my grandfather, living in his home, sleeping with his mother.

"Is Norman there?"

Dad was home, but my mother lied, instinctively protecting my father from what she sensed could be difficult news.

"Please tell him that his father is in the hospital. He's not doing well. He only has a few days left."

My mother didn't answer.

"Gloria?"

Rubbing the corners of her eyes with her left hand, she pulled the phone away from her ear, pausing to steady herself. "I'm sorry," she said. "I'm so sorry."

"And Gloria, there's one other thing." My mother could hear the caller inhale, a preparatory inward breath. "He's asking for Norman."

"Asking to *see* him?"

"Might there be any way Norman can get here?"

Again my mother paused, taking her own inward breath. "I don't know. I...honestly...don't know," she said, hesitating over each word. "I think I would have to talk to Norman about it."

My mother took down the hospital's address, the room number, and the name of the nurse on the floor in case it was needed. The phone call lasted less than two minutes.

Later that same day my mother told my father. He quietly listened, never saying anything, only looking away from her eyes to the floor and back again. For two straight days, as his father was fading away in a metal bed of white linens in the sterility of a hospital room, Dad gave no indication of what he might do—never asked for advice, never talked about it, never telephoned the hospital, the nurse's station, or his old friend.

On day three, something changed.

That morning, Dad drove himself to the hospital. My mother told me he took the elevator and asked the nurse where he might find his father. He stood outside the open door for several minutes, listening. The television hanging from the wall near the foot of the bed was tuned to what he believed was an old western movie, the volume just loud enough to detect the sound of gunfire. All Dad could see was the foot of the bed, a curtain drawn to conceal the man lying there.

"Can I help you?"

A voice called from behind him. He turned toward it.

"I'm a friend of the family," a young man said, reaching out his hand to shake my father's.

Dad didn't recognize the man, nor did he ask for any details of identity.

"I'm here to see my father," Dad said.

The man hesitated, puzzled by the words.

"I'm Norman."

"Oh. Yes. Norman," he said. "Let me check on your father. Tell him you're here."

Less than a minute passed before the man returned to the hospital room doorway.

"Go ahead in," he said.

I am sure Dad did not hesitate or second-guess his appearance. He likely walked into the room with a steady stride; maybe turning around just for a second to be sure the door closed behind him.

In the hallway on the other side of the door, hospital workers probably continued through their routines. Nurses with clipboards and metal rolling carts moved up and down corridors, and in and out of adjoining rooms. The phone rang at the nurses' station, and through the intercom system there might have been the request for the on-call doctor to report to the medical records office. A delivery man may have held a vase of daisies and asked a nurse's aide where he could find the room of the man whose name was printed on the attached card. And through the speakers on the wall there likely would have been the soft sound of music, maybe an orchestra's simple rendition of the Beatles' "Nowhere Man."

My father never talked about those fifteen minutes inside that hospital room. Never revealed what was said, discussed, or argued, if anything. There was never a word to anyone about apologies or blame, and never a suggestion of why he made the final decision to visit his father's deathbed. Dad was as silent about his father after his death as he was before it. And on the afternoon when the funeral home laid out my grandfather's body, Dad asked to attend on his own. His visit lasted only minutes. Dad signed the guestbook, knelt at the coffin to say a silent prayer, and left the viewing the same way he arrived, alone.

Many years later, my first son was born. I have this wonderful memory of my father holding Casey in his arms for the very first time in front of our home's fireplace, not unlike the fireplace in the old photograph. Dad is smiling. Casey is sleeping. My son did a lot of that. In fact, Casey entered the world seemingly at peace with it, barely making a sound. His mother, Marie, was frightened by the silence of his birth and startled the doctors and nurses with her shouts, "I can't hear him! I can't hear him!" She expected a cry, but Casey didn't wail when he arrived like most babies. The head nurse showed no immediate concern and did her best to ease Marie's anxiety. "He's just sleeping. A beautiful boy, sleeping."

The birth of my younger son, Graham, was an entirely different matter. I honestly believed I could hear gurgling in the birth canal in the moments before he was born, the sounds of a boy screaming to burst into the world. In fact, his long black hair—a highly unusual color and length for a newborn, nurses told us—arrived ahead of him. It hung out between his mother's legs, preceding the birth of the rest of his body. As my sons grew, I began to see how much their births matched their early personalities. Casey—controlled, calm, restrained. Graham—outspoken, emotional, artsy. And I loved being a father, watching them move through the stages of development and celebrating as their distinct qualities and characters emerged. I thought I was a pretty good father. But then Dad died. Prostate cancer. Unlike my father's experience, my relationship with my dad was a good one—complicated, yes—but good. Still, after his death, my view of fatherhood and of life began to shift and change. It no longer seemed easy. Naturally, like so many others who lose a parent, I tried to come to an understanding of my father's undeniable influence on my life, and how all that he was and wasn't had impacted my role as a man and as a father. I found myself reexamining long buried aspirations and dreams, reassessing my career and marriage, scrutinizing whether I was eating right, working out enough, feeding a suppressed spirituality. I reached to the past for comfort, returning to what my friends had called "my hippie days." I started playing guitar again, listening to music the way I did when I was an undergrad, discovering new music and new meanings in old Bob Dylan songs. And I was reading more. I devoured newer books like *The Four Agreements* by Miguel Ruiz and returned to old favorites like *Walden, Naked Lunch,* Hunter S. Thompson's *Fear and Loathing in Las Vegas,* and a book I read three times in a row in the summer of 1975 when I was nineteen, Kerouac's *On the Road.*

More than two decades later, I read Kerouac again, believing *On the Road* might kindle some old fires, start some new ones. I was forty-seven years old. The recognizable themes resurfaced in the book like the familiar stories school buddies repeat to one another year after year because the tales are always worth retelling. But there was also something new surfacing on its pages. As a man coming to grips with the death of his father, a divorce, a new career, and the inevitable realities of aging, I could see the possibilities for a new beginning. Although it's not in the published book, in the first sentences of the original scroll manuscript, Sal Paradise addresses his father's death, and I could certainly relate to that. Like Paradise, I longed for a new start. The similarities were striking. In the opening paragraph of the published book, Sal speaks of his "miserably weary split-up" with his wife and of feeling "everything was dead." I'm not sure I was that low. But I too had split-up with my wife, my career as a journalist had begun to feel like a "dead" end, I was trying to find my footing as an assistant professor at a college in Chicago, and when I looked in the mirror I saw an aging man who was completing a cycle of his life. Sal, although a far younger man, was in a parallel place when he left his writer friends in New York and headed west to meet with Dean and begin their road odyssey. He was ready for something new. But,

I'll admit, as a middle-aged guy, it wasn't easy for me to embrace this mantra. I might have had a kinship with Sal, but I wasn't Sal. I was no longer a young man, someone who could just put everything on hold, abandon convention. I was a grown-up. I had obligations to a job, a mortgage, and most importantly, I was the father of two boys. I had commitments to them, ones I wasn't about to walk out on. And I loved being a dad, even though I had found myself struggling to fully understand the role, especially in the aftermath of my father's death. So there I was once again, reading *On the Road*, but not acting on it, hoping its words alone would ignite something new, give me some answers, offer some purpose.

And then I found something that had escaped me as a nineteen-year-old.

Right there on the book's pages and nestled between the lines, is the theme of fatherhood. It comes up several times and in many ways. Sal and Dean search for Dean's "wino" father in Denver, but never find him despite Dean's tragic and estranged relationship with his father. Kerouac writes about the innocence of a father's protective love, asking why it's true that the early stages of life are many times forged by the beliefs we find under our father's roof. And throughout the road trip, you might say Sal is trying to find a surrogate father everywhere he travels, hoping for guidance from someone, something. And then there's that opening line in the original scroll manuscript where Sal tells the reader that his father has just died. In real life, Kerouac's father fell into alcohol and gambling, and died of stomach cancer a decade before *On the Road* was published, never knowing of his son's accomplishments. Undoubtedly,

David W. Berner

Kerouac's relationship with his father is part of *On the Road*, even if it's all in the shadows. These were my new discoveries in Kerouac's book. The wonderful inspiration *On the Road* once offered me as a teenager was blending with what I was now finding on its pages as an adult, reconnecting me with the story I loved. Maybe this new insight could somehow help free my head of the accumulated baggage of life, help me move forward from my father's death, and clarify my relationship with the fathers who came before me, the ones in that old photograph found at the bottom of the credenza drawer in my mother's home. Still, I wondered if I was putting too much stock in Kerouac's words. I wondered if rereading Kerouac was nothing more than silly nostalgia, like finding an old pair of bell-bottom jeans in the attic or the vinyl version of Deep Purple's *Machine Head* in a box in the garage. I certainly didn't want to trivialize what the book once meant and could mean again. So maybe I needed to take things a step further. Maybe I needed to take the plunge I was never brave enough to take when I was a young man. Maybe—just maybe—what I really needed to do was to get behind the wheel, to go on the road. Maybe now was the time to finally travel Kerouac's journey and take my two sons with me.

The photo of my father, my grandfather, great grandfather, and me now sits on a bookshelf in my home, the colors muted with age, the grainy visual texture more evident. And next to it is another photograph, a more recent one with truer colors and a sharp resolution—a photo of the digital age. The image is of my father standing chest-high in a swimming pool of chlorine-clear water, a summer destination. He's holding my oldest son when he was five-years old, bare-chested with droplets of water on their shoulders and foreheads, their sun-touched faces just inches apart, both smiling without anyone insisting they do so.

Chapter 2
Dents

ere's how I imagined it: a loosely planned five-thousand-mile road trip, beginning in Chicago, heading to Denver, San Francisco, Santa Fe, back to Denver, and then home to Chicago. And we would travel through some of the places and on the roads Kerouac wrote about. We wouldn't necessarily use *On the Road* like a map, there was no plan to go to New York or Mexico, but I did hope to travel on part of Route 6, a main westward artery when Kerouac took to the road. I considered heading out on my own; the trip might be more meaningful alone. But I also knew the emotional and even philosophical musings that sparked the idea were not unique. My friend Brad was just a few years younger than me, but very much in the same emotional place. Like me, he too had lost his dad. I had been through a change in careers—journalist to college professor. Brad had sold his restaurant business—a frozen custard shop—and was searching for a new direction. I recently had been divorced, so had Brad, and both of us were ready, especially at midlife, for a little self-discovery and the redemptive power of a road trip. And ironically, Brad lived in Denver, like Dean Moriarty.

But before taking to the highway, I wanted Brad to understand what this trip meant to me and how the spirit of a dead author and a more than fifty-year-old book helped fuel the idea. I told him about how the story had once inspired me. I told him about the old photograph I found, my uncertainties about how I was handling fatherhood, and how I believed Kerouac could be the perfect prescription for what I needed.

Brad, though, brought a completely different sensitivity.

"Jack, who?" he asked.

For Brad, this trip had little to do with the author and much to do with a middle-age adventure.

"Jack, Mac, Larry, Ed? Doesn't matter to me. I'm in."

Certainly the trip had deeper meaning for me, but in either case, *On the Road* was doing exactly what it had done to generations far younger—it was putting us behind the wheel.

In many ways this was a selfish endeavor. I was allowing myself, and now my friend, the time and space to make this three-week journey. Blocking out everything else in my life. Still, as a father of two teenage boys, I struggled with the thought of doing this without them. Giving up my time for theirs had always been part of the parental job description, so how could I take on what had the potential to be a memorable experience without sharing it with my sons? How could I not allow my younger son, thirteen-year-old Graham, to experience the beauty of such a trip—the camaraderie, the bonding? And how could I not allow fifteen-year-old Casey the chance to capture this journey through the lens of his camera? From the time he was six years old he was hooked on creating images, starting with 35mm disposable drug store point-and-shoots and progressing to a high-end digital Canon and a high-definition Sony video camera. He thrived on telling visual stories. It was what he wanted to do with his life, and he was already eyeing colleges with photography and film programs. There was no way I was going to leave him behind.

Casey and Graham heard me talk about the details of the trip, about my purpose for taking on the challenge of it, and an itinerary based on the travels written about in Kerouac's book. Although neither had heard much of anything about Kerouac, and neither was truly listening much to what they undoubtedly saw as Dad's self-absorbed enthusiasm for this writer and his book, they were willing to consider how there could be some teenage fun in these travels. I wanted them to feel every inch of the book's rebellious spirit, to understand that "Woodstock rises from its pages," as William S. Burroughs once said, and to know how this book will forever resonate with road trips everywhere.

Still, there was one very important question, and Casey got straight to the point.

"What would we be driving?" he asked.

I wasn't sure I wanted to tell him and the others what I had in mind. It was not exactly the romantic vision of the quintessential vehicle for a Kerouac inspired journey across the country.

I thought our best bet was to do it in a thirty-foot RV.

"Little lame, don't you think, Dad?" Graham said. I had taken all three of my fellow travelers to the RV rental office and allowed them to get a close-up look at the big box of a vehicle, walk around it, look inside it, and sit in the driver seat. Graham would rather we motored the roads in a $200,000 Lamborghini. Reading *Motor Trend* magazine produced high standards.

If I wanted to be true to the Kerouac spirit we would have found a vintage Cadillac or planned for highway hitchhiking and hopping trains, but none of that was a realistic alternative. Considering the logistics of this kind of travel, the RV made sense to me even if it wasn't quite like Jack.

"Graham, it's not about what we are journeying *in*," I said, resorting to a cliché, hoping the simplicity of it would resonate with a young teenager. "It's about the journey itself."

All of my fellow travelers needed some level of convincing.

"The choice of vehicle doesn't matter," I told Brad, who had come to Chicago for a summer visit and a look at the RV. "The book is our vehicle."

"I guess I have to read it now, huh?" Brad said, laughing.

"*On the Road*," I told them all, "is as cool as a 1965 Mustang convertible, a Porsche Roadster, or a brand new Harley."

Casey had his video camera with him and was pointing the lens inside and outside the RV. Although he didn't say a word while panning and zooming, I was happy about what he was doing. I told myself, even in his silence, capturing the RV through his lens was a level of acceptance.

"Maybe it's not very, *Kerouacian*," I said to Casey, trying to justify the use of one of the tackiest vehicles ever designed for travel. "But it *could* be cool, right?"

I knew I was desperately reaching.

"Dad, sorry," Casey said, hitting the pause button and pulling the camera down by his side. "This is a big tin can. It's *not* cool."

I rented one anyway.

Graham and Brad had come to see the benefits, even the potential fun of traveling in a "tin can." Casey obviously wasn't quite there yet. Initially, I think he was willing to listen to an argument for the RV and certainly understood the practicality of it, but wasn't ready to give in to what he likely saw as an old man's retirement home on wheels.

"The shower's bigger than I thought," Casey said, walking through the van with the video camera turned off. "And what's that?"

"That's an upper bunk," I said, patting my hand on the thin mattress to the bed perched above the RV's cab.

"Who's sleeping there?" he asked.

"Probably not you. You're too big." At fifteen years old, Casey was already more than six feet tall.

"Good. I guess I get the big bed then, right?" he said, smiling wryly.

"Guess so," I said, winking. I hoped giving him the back bedroom of the RV, the queen size bed and a private room, might win him over.

Casey and I shook on it.

Outside, Graham and Brad inspected the vehicle for scratches and dings, like you do when you rent a car at the airport.

"A couple nicks over here," Brad said, pointing to a rear wheel well.

"Dents here," Graham said, his fingers making circles around some blemishes on the driver-side door. "Looks like someone threw a baseball at the thing."

I laughed and noted it on the renter's inspection form. I had some history with wildly thrown baseballs and what they could do.

The white siding of my parents' home back in Pittsburgh where I grew up is covered with dozens of dents. Four or five pear-sized impressions surround the outside of the door to the backyard, and there are five or six other dings near the kitchen window. The more you look, the more you see: a bunch of them near the gutter that runs down the side of the house, a cluster just above the rose bush. This is the damage done by flying baseballs thrown from the untamed right hand of the neighborhood's worst pitcher.

"I'm over *here*, David. Right *here*," my father would say, pointing to his chest. Every time I'd whiz one over his head or several feet to the left and the ball would crash against the house, Dad would look right at me, locking his eyes on mine and say, "I'm right...*here*." He never said this with anger; it was more of a firm request. "Try to get it to *me*," he'd politely plead before stepping into the garden to retrieve the baseball that had left yet another permanent imprint on our house.

There's that old saying about a pitcher struggling with accuracy: *he couldn't hit the side of a barn.* I wasn't one of those pitchers; I had no problem hitting the side of the barn.

It wasn't that I hit the house with every pitch, but I hit it plenty, especially when I'd throw my SPOON ball. Unlike a fastball or curve (or the forkball), my SPOON required the pitcher to cup the ball with all of his fingers and the palm (like a spoon) and then just throw it as hard as he could. I had no clue how the ball was supposed to react, but I did know what usually happened: the ball would sail wildly out of control and as much as ten feet from my father's outstretched mitt. More than half of the dents in the siding came after I'd reached back and hurled my appropriately named, but highly ineffective, signature pitch. Surprisingly, I never broke a window. And through it all, Dad continued to urge me to throw with *just a little more accuracy*. Still, he never stopped playing catch, never encouraged me to give up the SPOON ball, and never suggested I should maybe try another sport, something less destructive, like badminton. But in the early 1960s, the boys in my neighborhood, the sons of strong-jawed working men who lived just over the river from Pittsburgh's steel mills, would never, ever, be caught playing badminton, even if one's baseball pitching skills could be considered public endangerment.

I played organized T-ball and Little League baseball up until my high school years. My pitching improved, but I was always just an average player. My sister was the real athlete. She ended up playing semi-professional softball. I ended up playing the guitar. Still, I loved the game, and many years later, when my two sons were young and we'd visit my parents in their little three bedroom house in the hills of Western Pennsylvania, I'd take the kids to the backyard to play catch. Occasionally they would throw a hardball or softball off the mark, hitting my parents' house, adding to the assortment of dents.

"No worries, boys," I'd say, "the house is already a pockmarked mess." Then I'd point to all the other dings. "See those? Those are your dad's. Every last one of them," I'd say, with a peculiar sense of pride.

"Dad, they're *everywhere*," the boys would say.

"Yep, I was learning on a very…long…curve."

When I said this to my sons, I could hear my father's voice. I sounded just like him, acted like him. I was being the same kind of dad as my dad, giving the boys a bit of instruction and then allowing them to wing it, to throw the ball as much and as far as they wanted. Each one of the old dents marked a moment in time when I was making mistakes, a lot of them. Dad didn't consider it damage; they were evidence of a starting point for progress. My father figured I would improve, sooner or later. But it didn't matter, really. He simply wanted to be there to watch me try to get better, dent-by-dent. The reason was simple: it was far more than his father ever gave him.

My father was not perfect. He had an unpredictable temper, and he could be moody, a personality trait he inherited from his father, I'm told. Still, Dad was determined not to make the kind of mistakes his father made. My father was not going to walk away from his family. He was going to go to the elementary school play, go to the middle school band concert, and play catch in the backyard even if it meant he'd have a house with smashed-up siding. Dad's fatherless childhood was why he based his entire philosophy of parenting on one thing: just be there.

That philosophy rubbed off on me. When I became a father, I too believed that being around was more than half the battle, a major part of the job. I had a role model for that kind of behavior. But, unlike my father's generation, the modern dad is much more of a hands-on kind of guy and that means more than just "being there." But more what? What is a modern-day father supposed to be? There are no clear answers, really.

It seems much of fatherhood is a mixture of hopeless guessing, ignored or ineffective discipline, a few hugs, and access to candy. Dads learn this messy process through trial and error, step-by-step. Face it. If you're a father, you're going to mess up. Just try not to do irreparable damage. When they're infants, avoid dropping them. When they're toddlers, try not to trip over them. And when they're teenagers, do your best not to kill them. Avoid gagging when changing a diaper filled with something outright beastly. And remind yourself that when it's all over your shoes, kid vomit is not dangerous biochemical waste, it is finely chewed-up Spaghetti-Os, a harmless puke. Be absolutely certain that when you're angry and you slip-up and say *fuck,* your son is going to repeat it, out loud…in church. Be secure in the likelihood that your boy will not be Tom Brady or LeBron James, but instead will probably need physical therapy for the malformation of his wrist due to playing 24-hours of Halo. Know that he won't tell you when he kisses his first girl on the lips, and certainly won't tell you when he moves onto other body parts. And if it's a guy he kisses, well, deal with it. Even embrace it. Be assured he won't send you an invitation to his first cigarette, first joint, first chug of Pabst Blue Ribbon, first Jack Daniels shooter. But try hard to be around if any of these become destructive habits. Be around to notice that when your son takes his first steps, he's stepping *away* from you not toward you. Know that when your kid is two years old, he'll learn to say *I love you, Dad.* And when he's sixteen, he'll learn to say *I hate you!* And it's undeniable that your son will see every single thing you do—the good, the bad, and the ugly. And he'll be taking notes, mental photographs. Sure, some of this is in

David W. Berner

the DNA and can't be helped, but the rest is observation that may be imitated, and imitation is not always the sincerest form of flattery, despite the believability of the old adage. Above all, know that there is no other relationship in the world that influences a man like the one he has with his father, no matter what kind of father he is. The absent fathers in *On the Road* aren't exactly role models, but they certainly make an impact. We are who we are because of the men who came before us. All the past interactions, the beautiful and the troubling in the long bloodline of fathers and sons are inextricably linked to the present and our all-too-often fruitless attempts to imitate the good and reconcile the ills of the man we call Dad.

My sister now lives alone in my parents' old house. She's never replaced or repaired the banged-up siding. That makes me happy. You see, at some point in a man's life, he will look in the mirror and see the reflection of his father. But for me, it's not always in the mirror where I'm likely to see Dad's image. Instead, it's in every one of those dents.

After another half-hour looking over the RV, I signed all the documents, wrote a deposit check for five hundred dollars, and made plans to return in less than a month to drive that big-ass vehicle, that tin can, off the gravel lot, and onto a westward highway.

Chapter 3
Are You Hitting on Her?

I stuffed a few final things in an old canvas bag, turned off the house's air conditioning, watered the Chinese evergreen and English ivy, and locked the red front door. It was just after sunrise when I took the short three-block walk to where the boys lived with their mother. I had parked the RV in front of Marie's home the night before and spent a couple of hours in the evening stuffing sleeping bags, lawn chairs, a few pots and pans, bath towels, and bed sheets into the various cubby holes and closets in the vehicle. I had also placed one of my newer hardback copies of *On the Road* on the dashboard.

The boys were still sleeping. Marie was making coffee.

"You ready for this?" she asked.

"I am *jacked,* so to speak," I said, grinning. It was a pun I had used before when talking about the trip. No one laughed anymore.

"Boys are going to need a little help understanding this Kerouac thing," Marie said. "They think you're talking about Jack *Kevorkian.*"

David W. Berner

Kevorkian was the pathologist who had become a right-to-die activist, and later was convicted of murder. He had helped more than one hundred terminally ill patients find a way to die.

"Oh, come on. They may not know Kerouac that much yet, but I think they know this trip is not based on Dr. Death," I said. "But, you know, Kerouac might have liked Kevorkian if he had known him. Old Dr. Death was a jazz musician, you know. Played the organ, I understand. Even had a CD out."

"How do you know stupid stuff like this?" Marie asked, shaking her head.

On the floor in the kitchen were two suitcases, identical black roller bags. One was not yet zipped shut. A white sock and the sleeve of a wrinkled tee-shirt hung out the side opening. On top of the other bag sat a computer and a spaghetti bowl of wires. It was easy to tell which bag went with which boy.

"Anything else they need to bring?" I asked, making a quick glance around the kitchen.

Before Marie could answer, I heard quick, heavy footsteps on the hardwood stairs behind me.

"Hey!" Graham always had good morning energy.

"Morning, my fellow traveler. Ready to roll?" I asked, putting my arm around his wide shoulders.

"I'm set," he said, hiking up his boxer shorts.

"Your brother up?"

I heard the shower turn on in the upstairs bathroom.

"There he is," Graham said, pointing toward the ceiling and the floor of the bathroom above.

"Question: You do know who Jack Kerouac is, right?" I asked.

"He's the writer guy."

"Yep. Not the suicide guy, right?"

"Suicide guy?" Graham scratched his bare belly.

Marie and I smiled.

Graham got dressed, the two of us tossed a few more things inside the RV, and then I started it up to get the air conditioning pumping. The morning was already steamy. Casey came downstairs and spent a few minutes pulling together his camera equipment and the remainder of his computer gear. Marie had put together a little bon voyage breakfast, so the four of us sat at the kitchen counter drinking coffee and juice, and eating sweet cinnamon rolls and bagels.

It was eight o'clock in the morning when I put the RV in drive and pulled away from the front of the house. Marie stood in the driveway waving, blowing kisses, and wiping tears from her cheeks.

It wasn't long before we were on the Illinois Tollway heading west. The boys were already settling in for a long drive. Graham sat in the passenger seat and Casey at the small table just behind the driver. I turned my head toward him.

"You do know Jack Kerouac is not the Dr. Death guy, right?"

"The suicide doctor? Oh, geez Dad."

"Just checking. Just checking."

Our plan was to drive through Iowa and arrive at the RV park near Omaha, Nebraska, around dinnertime. I had reserved a place there a few months before. It was about three hundred miles by highway from Chicago, but I wanted to get off the interstate and travel Route 6 for a bit, the road Kerouac hoped to take all the way across the country from Massachusetts to California. Plus, when we drove through Iowa, we needed some time to look for the prettiest girls in the world—and we weren't going to find them on I-80. Somewhere in the first part of *On the Road,* Kerouac wrote about all the beautiful women he saw in Des Moines. I joked with the boys that we should spend some time finding out if he was right. Of course, I didn't think women were any prettier in Iowa than they were anywhere else, or any prettier in Kerouac's day either. But a young man traveling by himself does get lonely, and when Sal Paradise was making his way through Iowa he was very much alone.

Route 6 led us to Walnut, Iowa. It was the first time I had negotiated the thirty-foot tin can around small town streets. With a sweaty forehead and tingling palms, I navigated the RV into a spot in a big parking lot behind Pearl Street, and we walked a couple of blocks to Aunt B's Kitchen. The sign on the old wooden door boasted a dozen varieties of pies.

"Apple, please," I said to the waitress, a woman with wavy gray hair pulled back in a messy short ponytail.

"Ice cream?" she asked in a quiet voice.

"Sure. Coffee too."

"And you, honey?"

"Apple," Graham said. "And lemonade, please."

I cringed at the peculiar combination of tart and sweet.

The waitress smiled at Casey.

"Lemonade. I guess apple is fine."

I cringed again. Only the young can mix the sweet with the sour.

"We do have a lot of others, sweetie." She was a kind woman with a soft, melancholy smile. She pointed to the menu, and Casey gave it another look.

"Where you fellas from?" It was something she surely asked anyone who wasn't a regular.

"Chicago. We're off on the first leg of a long trip. Going to San Francisco," I said.

"Oh, I have a sister in Chicago. Did you grow up there?"

"No. Actually I'm from Pennsylvania. Grew up outside Pittsburgh."

"You know Sharon, Pennsylvania?" Sharon was about an hour drive northwest of Pittsburgh. I had a college girlfriend who attended high school there. "I was born there," the waitress said.

"Sure," I said. "Reyers Shoes." Reyers was an enormous shoe store in Sharon. It was a destination for shoppers, an amusement park for people with a footwear obsession. The place had any kind of shoe you could imagine, hundreds lining the walls, and if they didn't they could order it.

"I know Reyers. Absolutely," she said, putting her hands on her hips.

"Did you happen to know the Routmans?" This was my old girlfriend's family name

"Routmans?" She tapped her pencil on her hip. "No, don't think so."

"Well, small world anyway, huh?"

"Sure is," she said, smiling that melancholy smile again. She was silent for a few seconds, seemingly considering what she may have left behind in Sharon, Pennsylvania—a childhood friend, a high school boy, a first love.

"Ya know, the apple is really okay," said Casey, breaking the quiet.

"Drink?" the waitress asked.

"Ah, the lemonade?"

"Oh sure," she said, remembering. "It'll just be a moment." She turned and put her hand on my shoulder. "And it was so nice talking to you."

When she stepped away, Casey and Graham rolled their eyes.

"What?" I said.

"Dad, why do you always have to talk to waitresses like they're your friends?" Casey said, smiling and shaking his head.

This was not a new question. We had been here before.

Not long before the road trip, I had the boys for the weekend. This was not the her-weekend-my-weekend-court-ordered-custody-agreement kind of thing; instead it was the can-you-be-around-for-the-boys-I'm-going-to-my-sister's kind of thing. There was no visitation order in the divorce. We hired a lawyer to make sure of that, believing we always would have enough respect for each other and our jobs as parents that we could amicably work it out without the courts. But if their mother knew I had taken the boys to Bar Louie that Friday night and was hitting on the waitress while they ate their potato-skin appetizer, she and just about anyone else would have been quick to question my parental judgment. Thing is, I wasn't really hitting on the waitress, at least I don't think so.

"What would you go with?" I asked. "The grilled salmon or the pork chop?"

The boys gave me that familiar roll of the eyes. Graham produced a mocking half-smile, and Casey's face turned red, his eyes looking down at the booth's fake leather seats to avoid any possibility of visual contact with the young woman sporting the tight white top and the low-riding jeans.

"Huh, well," the waitress said, leaning into me to point at the menu. Her perfume, musky and complex, moved over me like a wisp of an ocean wind, a little moist and salty. "I love the salmon. And you see here," she said, inching closer, her waitress' pencil touching the laminated menu, "it comes with garlic fries. Those are *super* tasty."

One of the straps of her top had fallen below her right shoulder, and when she bent over toward me, I got a peek of a tattoo, maybe a rose, just over her right breast.

"Perfect. I'll go with the salmon."

"You'll love it," she said, writing down the order and flipping her long bangs from one side of her face to the other in one quick movement.

"How 'bout you guys?" she asked, looking at the boys, her bellybutton now showing just above the waist of her skinny Urban Outfitter jeans.

"Burger, no lettuce or tomato," Casey said, looking at her just long enough not to be rude.

"Chicken fingers," said Graham, holding back a nervous laugh.

"Refill on drinks, guys?"

I asked for more water. The boys each ordered another diet Pepsi.

"Okay fellas," she said. "It'll just be a bit." She smiled, pushed the pencil into her front jean pocket, and then slid the order book inside the left back pocket, one of a pair that hugged the curve of her backside.

"You're gonna really like those fries," she purred, taking the menu from my hand.

"Lookin' forward to them," I said.

She flipped her bangs again and turned toward the bar, asking a customer sitting alone at a smaller table a few feet away if he was ready for a second Heineken. Then, when she was out of earshot, the boys gave it to me.

"Geez, Dad!" said Graham, holding the sides of his face with his hands like Edvard Munch's *The Scream*.

"Could it be more obvious?" said Casey, scolding me.

"Oh, for God's sake," I said. "I am *not* hitting on her." I found myself instinctively reacting to the boys the way I did when I was ten years old and my father caught me with his *Playboys*, each one opened up on my bedroom floor to photographs of airbrushed breasts. I frantically tried to shove the magazines under my bed while Dad stood there watching. It was a futile attempt to conceal a young boy's desire to ignite every one of his senses through his laser-like focus on the body of a woman. And now, decades later, I was once again attempting to muffle that hardwired truth.

"Dad, who asks the waitress questions like that unless you think she's hot?" said Graham, reveling in the belief that he had proof of his father acting inappropriately.

She *was* hot. Cute. Friendly. She was also half my age.

"Guys, I was just asking a question, being nice."

"Oh *sure*, Dad," said Casey, dismissing me.

I wondered at the time if the boys would have accused their father of this sort of behavior if the waitress didn't have that soft shoulder-length hair, that one-size-too-small top pressing against creamy skin, those jeans rounding around her thighs so snugly, that scent about her. Or maybe it was just simply where the boys and I were in our relationship—two young males paying more attention to a woman's hair, legs, eyes, and breasts, and their dad no longer married to their mother and considering, with plenty of self-imposed apprehension, dating again.

"Come on, guys. I'm not hitting on her." Then I moved a little closer and whispered, "But, if I was…well, she's pretty darn cute."

"Agh, Dad, stop!" said Casey, laughing uncomfortably. "You're like some *creeper*."

I leaned back into my seat, crossing my arms on my chest. I smiled. Graham interrupted the brief silence.

"Well, she *is* hot, Casey," he said, giggling and lifting himself up from the seat to look over the top of the booth, hoping to spot her.

"Graham! You're a freakin' pervert!" said Casey, pushing his brother back down in the seat.

"What if I *was* hitting on her?" I asked, attempting to seize what I thought might be an opportunity, albeit an awkward one, to combine a bit of male bonding with a teaching moment.

"See! I knew it!" Graham said, throwing his hands in the air.

"Not in front of us! Please!" said Casey, putting the palm of his right hand over his eyes. "Control yourself."

My sons were evolving right in front of me. The veil was slowly falling away from the concealed rawness of intimacy, revealing the boys' emerging awareness of youthful, visceral sensations. On the surface, what looked like two boys lightheartedly pleading with their father to curb what they believed was his overtly flirtatious conduct, was instead their attempt to conceal the chemical synapses of adolescence. There was no stopping this biology lesson. It was happening out in the open, in a bar, in front of everyone.

"Just because you are nice to a pretty lady, doesn't mean you want to rip her clothes off," I said, immediately feeling uncomfortable about what I had said and how defensive that must have sounded. *A father is not supposed to say that to his young sons, is he? But, it's true, isn't it? Ah, hell, I'm in deep now.* I tried harder to make my point. "Look, you guys think she's pretty, right? I know you do. You're boys. Young teenage boys. I was one. I know. I know what you're thinking."

"We certainly know what *you're* thinking," said Graham, looking at me with wide eyes, putting a forefinger to his cheek the way someone does when telling a secret.

"Okay, that's enough," said Casey, twisting anxiously in his seat.

Graham laughed and again peered over the top of the booth.

"It's okay, guys. Really, it's all right to express what you're feeling." As soon as I said this, the waitress appeared in my peripheral vision, her brown hair bouncing as she walked. I leaned in and whispered to the boys, "Just be respectful."

"Here're your drinks. Food should be up real quick," she said, placing the tall glasses on the table.

"Excuse me," said Graham unexpectedly. "Do my chicken fingers also come with those garlic fries you were talking about?"

"Not usually, but I can switch the order for you, sweetie."

Sweetie? Did she say sweetie?

"Ah, yeah, sure," Graham said, his cheeks instantly reddening.

"And how 'bout you?" she said, turning to Casey.

"I'm good, thanks," Casey answered, uneasily.

"Coming right up, guys," she said, again flipping her hair and pulling that slippery strap of her top up over her shoulder. She moved away from our booth, stepped into a perky, confident strut, then quickly stopped, backed up, and touched Casey on the arm. "We do have *cheese* fries?"

Casey looked at me, silently asking for his father's approval to switch his order and answer the attractive young woman who was now focusing all of her attention on him.

"Go for it," I said, grinning.

Casey gave her a shy smile.

"You got it, sweetie," she said, playfully tapping Casey on the upper arm and falling seamlessly back into the now familiar strut, speedily and expertly dancing around the handful of tables behind us, and disappearing through the door to the kitchen.

There was a beat of silence at the table.

Then, as if playing the role of a magnificently satisfied customer in an overacted theatrical performance, I said, "Isn't the service here just great?"

Graham pretended to faint, Casey's shoulders bounced in quick bursts, and both boys slapped their palms to their mouths, struggling to quiet the laughter exploding from deep in their guts.

The waitress at Aunt B's in Walnut, Iowa, was nothing like the one in Bar Louie, and the boys certainly knew that. Still, there was an awkwardness that emerged nearly every time their father was friendly with a woman, whether or not she was from Walnut, Des Moines, or Chicago, and no matter if she was or wasn't the prettiest girl in the world.

Chapter 4
Summer Swim

Fathers have chances to be heroes. You show up for all the Little League baseball games, fascinate by blowing smoke rings, mesmerize with a simple card trick, do that slight-of-hand thing where you pull a quarter from behind your kid's ear (my father did this all the time), or bring a brand new bike or Xbox up from the basement on Christmas morning. There are innumerable opportunities to do something they'll think is cool or save the day, giving them unexpected fun or a surprise smile. These moments usually happen when the kids are young and aren't expertly aware that their dad really didn't do anything all that special. But there are those times, even when your kids are jaded by the teenage years and absolutely certain their father is a complete idiot, you can still pull off something worthy of hero worship.

The RV park had a pool.

I didn't know that when I booked it, but acted as if I had planned it from the start. It had been a long day of travel for the boys, and a night of sitting around a campfire in a crowded RV park just wasn't going to cut it. The pool was perfect.

"Dad, do you know where my trunks are?" Graham asked, tossing clothes from his luggage bag to the RV's floor.

"Somewhere in that mess of a suitcase, buddy."

"The pool looks pretty decent," Casey said, standing on the top step of the RV's front door so he could see the pool over the high bushes surrounding the park's main building.

Graham, after giving up on the trunks and resorting to an old pair of shorts instead, jumped in first, splashing water up and out of the pool and over the white "No Running" message painted on the concrete. Casey grabbed a lounge chair and took a seat, opting to wait a few minutes before considering slipping into the cool water. I settled in with an old beat-up copy of *The Dharma Bums*. Besides *On the Road*, it was the only other book I brought along for the ride.

"Dad, you getting in?" Graham asked.

"Yeah, maybe."

"Oh come on," he pleaded.

"Not right now."

Instead, I read my book and checked the map again to see how long it was going to take us to get to Denver and pick up Brad. Now and then, I lifted my head to watch the boys. I'm not sure why I didn't get in the pool. I was unaware of it then, but I had made a mistake. I should have done a cannonball into that pool, right between my two sons, soaking them with a mighty splash of chlorine-heavy water. Just finding the park with a pool wasn't enough to merit full hero status. I needed to go all the way; I needed to get wet. Sal Paradise saw Dean Moriarty as his hero, a symbol of the untamed American West. But, in the end, after thousands of miles on the road, Dean fails to live up to Sal's hero worship, and Sal sadly realizes heroism is a lie. Still, for me, there were those beautiful moments as a boy when my heroes were a clear and perfect truth.

We hit the highway early the next morning—all of us slow, sleepy, and quiet—and I promised myself if there were other pools in other RV parks, I would be the first to jump in.

Swimming was a big part of my growing up. A few times a summer, Mom would stuff the car with kids from the neighborhood, and we'd head for an afternoon at the municipal pool. Boys and girls would be sitting on the car's floor and on each other for the five-mile drive. There were no seatbelt laws, of course, and no one seemed to care that a four-door sedan was bulging with unbuckled little bodies. But what I remember most was when Dad would assemble our little backyard pool, spending hours on an early spring day to get it ready.

"Pull the hose around the tree and up close here," Dad said. It was one of those unseasonably warm Sunday afternoons in mid-May we were sometimes blessed with in Pennsylvania.

I was eight years old, impatient for summer, impatient for the pool. I was already in my royal blue bathing suit, my cherubic belly protruding over the white drawstring tied too tightly at the middle of my waist.

"When you get it up here, go back and turn the water on, but only when I tell you." Dad tried to direct this project with simple commands.

The metal section of the pool had been rolled up and stored away in the garage for nearly nine months. It took two people to stretch out the thin, steel outside wall of the pool onto the backyard grass and wash it down with water from a hose.

41

David W. Berner

I ran over the lawn and walkway, navigating my sensitive, shoeless feet around the cracks in the stone that lined the ground to the outside faucet. I was nearly shivering in anticipation of the first swim of the season. I put my hand on the knob and peeked around the corner of the house, poised for the next command from Dad.

"Hold on, get back here," he said. "I still need you to help roll out the liner over the grass."

How long is this going to take? I slumped back to Dad. It was now clear to me constructing our pool was not going to happen at the speed any young boy would have hoped.

The blue liner, nearly matching the color of my bathing suit, was a thick, heavy, flexible plastic or rubber of some kind. It, like the metal, had been put away for the winter and needed a bath. When we unfolded it, there were two or three spiders inside and a dead moth.

"We're going to need a little soap on this," Dad said. "Go ask your mother for a small cup of laundry detergent."

Now he needs soap? The pool set-up was becoming a far more laborious job than I would have liked. This was not what I expected. Instead of getting closer to a swim, it seemed further away than ever. I took the long way into the house, stopped at the refrigerator for a drink of milk from the bottle, grabbed a cookie from the cupboard drawer, and paused to pet the dog, a six-year old Collie.

"Mom?" I yelled from the kitchen, kneeling on the floor, my hand still on the dog's head between her ears.

My mother appeared from the basement stairs.

"Dad needs soap for the pool," I told her, my eyes and hand fixed on the dog.

She reached under the sink and pulled out a large box of Tide and poured about two inches worth in a plastic cup. I gave the dog a few more pets, grabbed another cookie from the cupboard drawer, and walked the soap to the backyard.

"Where've you been, for God's sake?" Dad stood near the blue liner with his hands on his hips, the hose hanging over his shoulder. "You want to swim or not?"

I didn't say a thing as Dad snapped the cup out of my hands. "Did you bring a scrub brush?" he said.

"You want one?"

Dad rolled his eyes and slapped the palm of his hand on his forehead.

I turned and ran to the door to the kitchen. "Mom?"

"Jesus, Mary, and Joseph." My father said the Biblical names in a stiff, staccato beat, shaking his head and launching into a quiet laugh.

I rushed out of the kitchen to the outside, the screen door slamming behind me, hoping to ease Dad's irritation with my lack of focus by quickly retrieving what he needed.

"Scrub brush, Dad," I said, dutifully handing him what Mom had given me—the brush with the large handle and the worn, coarse bristles on the one end.

He took it, said nothing, and again shook his head.

I didn't want to make him angry, so I waited a few more seconds before I asked the question.

"How long to do you think, Dad?"

"Oh for Christ sake," he laughed. "Go turn on the hose."

This time I didn't hurry. It seemed that rushing wasn't helping me get any closer to the cool waters of a backyard pool. I walked to the outside faucet as if I were walking to my school—a slow, meandering pace interrupted only for a second to kick an early season dandelion.

"Jesus, David, take your finger out of your ass!"

Finger out of my ass? It's not IN my ass.

"I would like to get this done before August," my father crackled, his voice unsympathetic and rougher than before.

I started half-running, a visceral response to avoid verbal punishment. And I felt my face flush. *Did I have my finger up my ass? Why would I do that? I have never heard of someone with their finger up their ass.*

I turned the faucet knob and waited for my father's next command.

"Good," he yelled from the yard. "Stay there until I tell you to turn it off."

I stood alone, out of Dad's sight, trying to figure out what in the world he meant. *Finger up my ass?* Obviously, the subtleties of understanding figurative language were still years away.

"Turn it off," Dad yelled. "But don't move."

Should I ask him? I can't ask him, can I?

"Okay, turn it back on."

I heard the scrape of the brush on metal and the rush of water, and leaned against the aluminum siding of the house, still out of Dad's sight.

Who would put their finger up their ass?

"Okay, turn it off. We're done," Dad shouted.

The clean-up was over, and when I returned to the yard Dad was already shaping the metal walls of the pool into a circle, snapping the ends together to create a round shape two feet high and twenty feet around.

"Grab that end of the liner and help me lift it over the edges," Dad ordered.

The pool was beginning to take form as Dad worked his way around the circle, connecting the long plastic rim that held the liner to the metal.

"How long will it take to fill it up?" I asked, hoping somehow my question would give what felt like a plodding, tedious timeline a bit of a boost.

"I don't know. Couple hours?" Dad said, staying focused on his work and continuing to snap the plastic rim into place.

Couple hours? Jesus, Mary, and Joseph. I kicked another dandelion.

Eventually, Dad fell into a rhythm, snapping his way around the circle with a certain tempo. He even began to whistle.

"Dad?" I asked.

"What is it?" he said, suspending his version of Johnny Cash's "Ring of Fire" just long enough to respond.

I can't believe I'm actually going to ask this.

"What did you mean about—finger up the ass?"

"What?" Dad said, halting the job for a moment to look straight at me.

"What you said—finger in my ass—what do you mean?"

Dad stopped snapping and from a crouched position he turned and sat on the grass, put his arms on his knees, and asked, "You're serious?"

David W. Berner

My face flushed again, just as it did before. And again, Dad shook his head.

"It's nothing, David," he said, beginning to chuckle and return to the work of fastening the liner. "I just got a little frustrated, a little impatient. Forget I said that."

I smiled not knowing exactly why.

"Well," I said, "just so you know. I did *not* have my finger up my ass."

His chuckle erupted into to a full, hearty laugh, as if someone just delivered the punch line to his favorite joke. I smiled. Again, not knowing exactly why. Then Dad wiped a few beads of sweat from his forehead with the back of his right hand.

"You really are something, David," he said.

I thought for just a moment—*I'm really something*—what does that mean? But I quickly dismissed the question. In front of me was a nearly assembled pool, and I finally began to truly believe the first summer swim was actually going to happen.

"Dad?" I asked. "You gonna swim with me later?"

Through his waning laughter, between the inhales and exhales, he said, "There isn't anything that sounds better. Not a single thing." He snapped the final foot of the liner rim in place. "Let her rip."

I ran to the faucet, twisting my body so I could reach my hand behind me, and yanked the bathing suit bottom out from between the cheeks of my buttocks. *Is this what he means? Finger in my ass?* I jumped over the walkway stones, keeping my bare feet from the uneven ground. I nearly fell down from my unbridled eagerness and had to grab hold of the faucet knob to keep my balance. I used both hands to turn it counterclockwise and immediately began to hear the rush of water inside the long green garden hose. Inch by inch, water made its way to the bottom of the blue liner, creating the sound of soft splashes in the late afternoon air.

Chapter 5
First Shot

I wanted to blink my eyes and be in Denver. Just like Sal Paradise, I longed for the Mile High City. That's where my friend was waiting; that's where there would be Kerouac and Beat haunts to see, *On the Road* bookmarks. I decided to get an early start out of Nebraska and try to make Colorado as quickly as possible. Rushing it seemed to go against the Kerouac spirit, but Paradise was in an enormous hurry to get to Denver from his aunt's home in New Jersey, so my impatience was not unlike his. Sal wanted to experience the West, and he dreamed of Denver every step of the way.

But there was still plenty of road to burn.

Nebraska is a boring state. It's flat and tired and worn.

"Are we in Colorado yet?" Graham asked.

"Nope. Coming up on Grand Island," I said, wondering why a western town built on dusty earth would be called an island. Maybe it's the isolation that appeared to surround this part of the country, a lonely solitude. Kerouac wrote about sad people and places throughout *On the Road*. His characters longed for deep personal, even spiritual connections, and when they didn't get it, sadness enveloped their souls and spilled out on the land where they traveled. Kerouac infused melancholy into his description of one particular night drive through Iowa, but it could have been Grand Island, Nebraska.

We crossed the state line, moved into the northeast tip of Colorado and through the barren, tumbleweed towns of Sedgwick and Crook. Sagebrush, rocks, and an occasional wooden or wire fence divided the land. It looked like ranch country, but for one hundred miles we never saw a cow or horse, and not one human being, except in an occasional passing car.

I grew up in the leafy hills of western Pennsylvania. And although there was plenty of wild nearby—pine and oak forests, quick streams, and overgrown trails—what we were seeing now was far different. Northeast Colorado was a heartbreaking landscape with its own melancholy beauty. I could imagine a cowboy, a modern-day Dean Moriarty, walking alone over the brown earth, denim shirt and jeans, and a rifle in his hand, firing at a rabbit or coyote just for sport. He would never say a word; never celebrate his marksmanship. Instead, he'd quietly walk to stand beside his victim, squat down to examine its condition, touch its lifeless body, and slowly move away, reloading his weapon and again surveying the land before him. This is what a man did in northeast Colorado. It is what his father did and all the fathers before him. It was a hunter's bloodline, and I knew a little something about that.

I was ten years old when Dad wanted me to shoot. Aim and pull the trigger. He decided it should be a shotgun, something he knew a good deal about. He kept two inside a cabinet in the basement, and on this afternoon he had lifted one from its rack—a break action single-barrel shotgun, the kind that hinges in the middle. His thick fingers wrapped around the forestock, and he carried it with the barrel pointed toward the ground. He said it was the safest way to hold a firearm. The shotguns were always under lock and key, and always unloaded. But now, one was out from behind the gun cabinet's glass door, and there was a shell in its chamber.

"Every boy should know how this feels," he said, walking with the confidence of a celebrated big game hunter, Hemingway-esque, to the top of the hill of our front yard beside the big evergreens near the front entrance to the house. I was a step or two behind him, watching the shotgun rock in his right arm as he moved. Dad knew about guns. He'd been around them all his life, and he believed it was time his son knew about them, too.

Across the street were dense woods where gigantic cherry trees towered over smaller locusts and maples. Deer would occasionally run up over the ravine after drinking from the creek in the valley, and neighborhood kids would play army, cowboys and Indians, and hide-and-seek in the thick brush and on the trampled trails.

"You're going to shoot this shotgun into the woods," Dad said. "You'll aim it high, way up at the top of the trees, and pull the trigger."

I had been curious about the firearms Dad kept in the basement. It was hard not to be when they were so unavailable, so off-limits. Dad only opened the cabinet to occasionally clean the weapons. He didn't hunt as much anymore, not like he did when he was a younger man. Nearly every weekend,

Dad used to stalk deer, turkey, rabbit, pheasant, and even fox in the woods around us. Pennsylvania was a hunter's state. The high schools were empty on the first day of deer season, venison was wrapped and frozen in refrigerators every fall, and manhood was measured by the points on the deer antlers you had mounted in your house.

The hunting gene didn't make it into my DNA. I have no idea why not, but I certainly would never have openly admitted it. In my hometown in the late 1960s, suggesting that you were not a fan of guns, not a hunter, and did not feel the need to put a bullet into Bambi or Peter Rabbit would undoubtedly provoke serious ridicule from your friends and maybe your own father. I never asked to shoot any of Dad's guns, but I wonder now if his insistence that a young man must experience firing a weapon was rooted in nagging guilt. By the time he handed me that shotgun, he had virtually abandoned his once weekly, almost ritualistic hunting adventures, taking up woodworking and golf. But everyone else around him had been a hunter their entire lives—his neighbors, his friends, his father-in-law, and his own father. It was what all the men around him did. This may have been on Dad's mind that day. But for me, standing on the hill in the front of our house with a loaded weapon, there was only one thing to consider: why in the world would we want to release a shower of shot pellets into the woods where my friends and I sometimes spent our summer afternoons?

"Dad," I said. "Couldn't we hit somebody?"

"Oh, you're not going to hit anyone," he said, quickly dismissing me. "Now, stand right here and grab it with both hands."

I stepped toward him in the middle of the yard's highest point and clumsily placed my hands around the stock and the barrel. The shotgun was far heavier than I thought it would be.

"Don't drop it," Dad said. He guided my right hand toward the trigger guard and placed my left on the wood underneath the barrel. "You got to hold it right." The metal was cold and the wood smooth and polished. "Now, this part," Dad said, touching the stock with his index finger, "this is what you have to keep tight against that little crease where your right shoulder meets your chest." He pushed the butt of the shotgun against me. "Do *not* forget that. You hear me?" he said, looking me in the eye. I didn't answer. "Okay?" he asked again, grabbing my chin and forcing me to look at him.

"Okay," I said.

"I'm serious. Just…like…this." He pushed the butt tighter into my shoulder.

When Dad was a boy, maybe about ten years old, his brother—twelve years his senior—was schooling him on how to shoot a shotgun. Dad's father had no interest in or patience for teaching my dad how to shoot. So, my uncle stepped in. He told my father it was critical to keep the butt end of the shotgun two inches *away* from his shoulder. *You have to leave a little space in there,* he told him. *It's important,* he said. When Dad fired his first shot, the kick launched his body backward, knocking him violently to the ground. The force threw the shotgun over Dad's head and into the nearby brush. The vicious crash of the butt against his shoulder left a black-and-blue mark that took weeks to heal. His brother laughed. Dad never forgot.

"This tight enough?" I asked.

Dad grasped the barrel and gave the shotgun another shove into my shoulder.

"See the tops of the big trees?" Dad said. "That's where you'll aim." He told me to look straight down the barrel toward the blue sky just above the highest branches, and then he took the index finger of my right hand and placed it on the trigger. "How's that feel?"

"Okay," I said nervously. "It's okay."

Dad reached behind the trigger guard and switched off the safety. *Click.*

"What was that?" I asked skittishly.

"It just means you're ready to shoot."

"Okay."

"But not yet," Dad said, quickly realizing he may have inadvertently given the go ahead. "Don't pull the trigger. Don't do anything."

"Okay."

"Do *not* pull that trigger," he blurted.

"Okay."

"You looking down the barrel?"

"Yes."

"Aiming above the trees?"

"Uh, huh."

"Butt right up against your shoulder?"

"Yes."

Everything now seemed incredibly quiet. It was as if someone had turned down Earth's volume, shutting off the singing birds and the breeze that swayed the branches of the front yard evergreens. Then, the stillness was broken.

"Stop!" Dad yelled.

"Dad?"

"Do *not* shoot!"

I was frozen, my eyes fixed on the sky above the trees, the barrel still angled upward, and my finger on the trigger.

Down the street, just past the large cherry tree that loomed over part of our front yard, I could hear the sound of an engine. A car was beginning its ascent up the hill and in just a few seconds would travel in front of us, just below the sight of the shotgun, only degrees from what was to be the shell's trajectory. Dad put his hand on the barrel and slowly pushed it toward the ground as both of us silently watched the car pass, the driver apparently unaware he was crossing in front of an armed man, and an armed boy.

"Okay, aim it again," said Dad as the car traveled out of sight.

I hesitated and looked at my father.

"Come on," he said, "before there's another car."

Again, I looked down the barrel, aiming high above the trees, pressing the butt against my shoulder.

"Got it?" Dad asked.

I nodded.

"Now, pull the trigger," he said. "Sort of squeeze it."

I don't remember for sure, but I can bet the index finger of my right hand was trembling.

"Go ahead," Dad said, believing I must not be pulling the trigger with enough force. "Squeeze it."

It took a split second to fire the shotgun. But in that flash of time, every distinctive stage of the process of shooting was somehow elongated. There was the click of the trigger, the metal-to-metal clack of the shell falling into place, and the heat manufactured on the forestock from the friction of the shell rocketing through the barrel. These occurred in individual stages, each one as clearly defined as the next. Then, pure power took over. The shotgun snapped backward, its butt jamming into my body, the barrel lifting skyward. And suddenly there was the warm pungent smell of gunpowder swirling in the air. I tried my best to stand as motionless as possible. Instead, my hands shook and my legs wobbled.

"Whatta ya think?" Dad asked.

"It's loud," I said softly, lowering the shotgun's barrel, still taking in what had just happened.

Dad smiled and took the shotgun from my hands.

"Did I hit anything?" I wondered, looking anxiously at the woods.

"Besides just missing that car, I don't think so," Dad said, grinning. He was clearly pleased with the way things had gone. I was not so sure.

For weeks afterward I thought about that single shot. I wondered about the driver in the automobile. *Did he see me with the shotgun? Did he tell someone? Did he alert the police? And what about my friends who played along the trails just behind the big cherry trees? Were any of them there? Did they hear the shot? Did they hide? Duck the buckshot? And the deer in the woods? What did they do? Scatter in fear when the blast broke the silence? And up in the trees, did the birds fly away fast enough when the pellets came raining down?* For days I was uneasy, worrying that a single ball of lead may have pierced its way through the sky, embedding itself in the breast of a robin, sending its body tumbling from the cherry trees to the underbrush.

It was a long time before I returned to those woods to play. And I have never again pulled the trigger of a gun.

Denver was just in front of us now. I could nearly touch it. Graham watched a movie on the computer, Casey aimed his video camera at the road sign marking the mileage to Colorado's biggest city, and I dialed my cell phone to connect with Brad, pick a place to meet so he could lead us to his apartment, and settle in for three full days in the city that was the nucleus of Kerouac's story. And although we were following the rough plan of a road map, a predetermined route, somewhere in a dusty corner of Colorado it became clear how irrelevant any map really was. A couple of years before he died, George Harrison sang a song in a surprise acoustic performance on VH1. It was just George and his guitar. The lyrics to *Any Road* emerged from my memory as if illuminating the pavement in front of me, words about taking a road, any road, to find out where you're headed. Yes, I wanted to stay true to Kerouac's travels, but it really didn't matter if I did or not. Any road would take us where we were going.

Chapter 6
Dope

I t was in Key West that Brad and I decided to buy scooters. Months before the Kerouac road trip, I was hired to review a resort and golf course in the Florida Keys for an online publication. It wasn't the kind of writing I loved, but it paid well, and it meant a trip to the semi-tropics and out of Chicago's bitter winter. I asked Brad to come along, as he'd always been a good sidekick. The two of us rented mopeds for a few days and rode them everywhere. One late night, after far too many shots of Jameson and Brad's numerous unsuccessful attempts to make the waitress at Sloppy Joe's, we drove the scooters through the narrow Key West side roads, avoiding Duval Street and the omnipresent Saturday night cops, on our way to our rented cottage not far from the Hemingway house.

"We got to get a couple of these," Brad yelled to me at a stoplight, smacking the handlebars of his two-wheeled fun ride.

"Your blinker's still on," I said, raising my voice above the noisy two-stroke engines.

"What?"

"Blinker. Turn signal."

We had made a left turn before the stoplight and had planned to go straight through the intersection, but on a scooter the turn signals are manual, so there it was, a single yellow signal, blinking away.

"Oh, yeah," Brad said, flicking it off.

It was the fourth time I had to tell him to turn off his blinker.

"Nothing like a flashing light to signal the police that there's a drunk guy on a moped," I said, laughing.

We made it back to the cottage at 3:00 a.m. It was mid-afternoon before our first cup of coffee.

The memory of that night fueled the purchase of a couple of scooters in the spring, and when we arrived in Denver in the RV, it was Brad on his new ride who met us at the Park Avenue exit off US-87.

"There he is," Casey said, pointing through the windshield. He spotted Brad sitting backward on the moped, facing oncoming traffic.

"Oh geez, he has his scooter," Graham laughed. The boys had nothing against the Vespa-like vehicles. They liked riding mine. But their father or his buddy Brad on a scooter? That was different.

"And he has those hipster sunglasses on," Casey said.

They liked Brad, but the boys clearly believed men of a certain age should act a certain age.

Brad waved us toward the road just off the exit. We drove behind him a few miles, watching his turn signals for clues where to go, and followed him to his apartment in a historic old building on what used to be the Lowry Air Force base.

"Son-of-a-bitch. You finally made it," Brad said as I stepped out of the RV's cab.

"Two days. A steady ride," I said, reaching back in to grab *On the Road* from the dashboard. "Here. Maybe you can read this while we're here."

"Oh yeah. This trip is connected somehow to this Jack guy, right?" he said, playing dumb.

We stood outside the RV, and Brad asked the boys about the vehicle. What was it like to ride in? Sleep in? How was the shower? They told him about forgetting to hook up the water line the first night at the campground, trying to maneuver the unwieldy vehicle on the narrow roads in the RV park, and the outrageous cost of gas.

"How's it to drive?" asked Brad.

"You sit high and never realize you have all that footage behind you," I said. "And you certainly feel the damn wind."

"Well, *I'm* taking it through the Rockies." Brad had been in Denver for years and knew the mountain highways.

The boys smiled. They had seen Brad drive before, been in the car with him, and knew there'd be a little thrill in each turn.

We spent the evening on Brad's deck, mapping out our planned Denver stops: Larimer Street where Dean Moriarty lived in a cold water flat, Charlie Brown's grill at the Colburn Hotel where Kerouac and Allen Ginsberg hung out, and Sonny Lawson ball field in the Five Points area, the one-time Harlem of the west with its 1940s jazz clubs where Kerouac was said to have watched softball games and took notes for *On the Road*. After offering Brad some background on why Denver was so important to Kerouac and its connections to *On the Road*, he began to show more interest in the book and the man who inspired this trip. Brad had some questions: What was his first book? What about his poetry? When did he die? Was he really on the old Steve Allen Show? Brad loved Denver, had made it his home after growing up outside St. Louis and living in Atlanta and Chicago, and talked about his adopted city like a paid representative of the tourism bureau. What he didn't know was how Kerouac and other writers and poets fit in to the Denver story. And he knew nothing about the so-called Beats, their lust for life, their disdain for conformity.

"I think I would have loved hanging out with those guys," Brad said. "Can you imagine sitting in a bar all night with that bunch? The drink, the drugs, the women."

"Yeah," I laughed. "But they did some great writing, you know?"

"They were living on the edge."

The discussion was familiar. I'd had this talk with colleagues, friends, and family numerous times. Why is it that so many artists believe it a necessity to break the rules of convention, to seek substances in order to distort what's real? What is it about creative people? Van Gogh, Jackson Pollack, Dylan Thomas, Hemingway, Faulkner, F. Scott Fitzgerald, Kerouac were all troubled, unstable, off-balance. Some had mental problems; many were drinkers, drug users. Their work was infused by their disturbed minds or the intake of pot, whiskey, beer, gin, or cheap wine. Drugs and drink are everywhere in *On the Road*, creating a hazy lens through which its characters see reality. Human beings have always adjusted, enhanced, and muddied their view of the world with hallucinogenic vegetation, stiff cocktails, smoke from pipes, man-made chemicals. Sal and Dean were no different. At times, they believed pot—they called it "tea"—was more important than food, more enlightening than God. Sal smoked the grass Dean bought in New York and claimed it allowed him to think freely, see things more clearly. Somewhere in each of our lives, just like Sal, we have all glorified the altered state.

A couple of years after our road trip, the subject of drink and drugs came up again, and this time it was personal.

There was a familiar sound at four o'clock every weekday afternoon in the home where my sons lived. The thud of the storm door from the garage into the kitchen signaled that Casey had returned home from his high school classes.

"You've read *The Sun Also Rises*, right?" he asked, skipping right past any attempt at a simple hello.

"And, how was your day?" I asked from my seat in the brown leather chair in the family room. His mother was out-of-town and I was staying at her house for a few days to be close to the boys, commuting to my teaching job at the college and occasionally working from home.

"It's one of your favorites, right?" Casey's question seemed a little like an accusation.

"Big Hemingway fan, and that one is probably the novel I love the best," I answered.

"I don't get it," he said, dropping his school backpack on the kitchen floor, shaking off his jacket, and tossing it over a kitchen chair. "It's just a bunch of people, with seemingly no jobs, drinking, having sex, and acting all self-important."

"Yeah, that's about it," I said, laughing. "But it's so well told. How far you in?"

The Hemingway classic was one of several books Casey was assigned to read in his advanced literature class. "And did you figure out what's wrong with the main character, Jake?"

Casey, searching the refrigerator for the carton of cranberry juice paused for a moment, and then he squinted his eyes, pointed to his crouch and said, "His *thing* doesn't work?"

"Yep, his *thing* doesn't work. But don't you see how Hemingway weaves that into the story? He's a master at revealing details with only the slightest bit of information. You have to read the short story 'Hills Like White Elephants.'"

Casey rolled his eyes. "You're obsessed."

"You should know Hemingway. You should read him."

"I *am* reading him," Casey said. "I still don't get it."

"You'll see the appeal. It'll take time, but you'll see it," I said. "You know he was born in Oak Park?"

"Yeah, Dad, I know," Casey said. He was exhausted by the zillions of times I had pointed out to him little facts about Hemingway's birthplace in the Chicago suburb; the zillion times I told him about his writing, his legend. "And I know he wrote about fishing in Michigan, and he lived in a house in downtown Chicago for a time, and the house now has a plaque on it, and he lived in Paris, and he was an ambulance driver in Italy, and he lived in Cuba, and he liked bullfights, and he drank a lot, and he shot a lot of lions and elephants, and he blew his brains out. Yep. Got it, Dad."

I was easily worked up when I talked about writers and poets. Sometimes I would become emotional when I read their words to the boys, or talked about their impact on literature. I cried when I saw Hemingway's writing room at his home in Key West. The tour took me through the main house and then back to a detached room in the rear of the property. Hundreds of books were neatly positioned on simple white shelves. A white Rolodex and two short stacks of books lay on a round table with ornate legs, and at the table's edge sat a grey portable manual typewriter with a sheet of white paper tucked inside its roller, as if it were waiting for a pair of hands to tap at its keys.

"And another thing," Casey added. "What's with so many writers being drunks or killing themselves?"

"Like who?" I asked, wanting to know what he already knew.

"Hemingway, that Fitzgerald guy, Kerouac. Didn't they all, like, drink themselves to death or something?"

"Pretty much."

"Then there's Poe who was an opium addict, I think," Casey continued. "And Eugene O'Neill. Jeez. He was an alcoholic. We read *Long Days Journey into Night* earlier this year. God help me. It was the most depressing story I've ever read in my life."

"Bit of a downer," I said.

"Was there any writer who wasn't screwed up?"

"Your dad," I said, laughing.

"Oh, I don't know about that," Casey said.

"Come on, really? Do you see me swigging out of a bottle of Southern Comfort right now?"

"Give it time," he said, smiling. "Give it time."

"I wonder," I said, "do you think artists, true artistic geniuses, have demons? And are the demons necessary to be brilliant?"

Casey held the cranberry juice carton up to his mouth, his right hand's index finger indicating to wait a moment. I kept talking.

"Look at Van Gogh or Jackson Pollack. Look at Dylan Thomas. Look at some of the rock legends—Kurt Cobain, Jimi Hendrix—even John Lennon had his drug issues. James Taylor was a heroin addict. Then there's Charlie Parker and Miles Davis."

Casey took a breath between gulps. "But not every artist is a nutcase or hooked on drugs. Some are, like, *normal*," he said.

"Yeah, but the normal ones are not so interesting, are they?"

"So, you believe that to be interesting you have to be a mess?" Casey said, challenging me.

"Well, I think we're all complex, don't you?"

"So, how much dope did *you* smoke?"

"Dope? Me?"

"No one else in the room."

I should have expected the question. Casey never hesitated to give his opinion, challenge a friend, a teacher, or his parents. *Question authority*, I would say. *Ask why*, I would say. *Hold people accountable,* I would say.

"I smoked it twice, both times in college. Did nothing for me."

"Oh, come on! Parents say that all the time."

"It's true."

I told him about a party at a friend's apartment off campus and how someone handed me a joint, how I took two puffs and felt nothing. Then I told him about the time I was in a rock band in college, and we were recording in a small studio on campus. One of my friends worked in the broadcast department and had a key to the place. We snuck in on the weekend and recorded two songs. Then, afterward, we smoked from a shared pipe. I took two, maybe three hits.

"I don't know," Casey said. "Maybe there's something about the creative process. Maybe it encourages you to be... hedonistic?"

"Are those people in *The Sun Also Rises* hedonistic?" I asked. "They are certainly lost souls, uncertain of what makes them happy. But hedonistic? I wouldn't call it that. Creative? Yes."

"Well, Jake is sort of creative. But maybe because he can't use *it*," said Casey, pointing to the zipper of his trousers, "he drinks a lot. He drinks so he can be creative or maybe *because* he's creative."

"Maybe that's worth discussing in your class," I suggested, reaching for the cranberry juice carton. Casey was now pulling textbooks and notebooks from his backpack. He was apparently finished with our conversation.

"And you?" I asked, taking a sip of juice. "Smoked dope yet?"

He lifted his eyes from inside his backpack.

"Ah, *no*."

"Maybe that's why you're not very creative?" I said, joking.

"Oh, shut up," he said, reaching again for the juice carton. "Go away. Don't you have to go smoke some dope or something?"

We both laughed as he tipped the carton toward his lips.

"Hey!" Casey said, turning the container upside down, the spout pointing toward the kitchen counter. "Thanks for drinking all of it!"

"You're welcome," I said.

Two years after Casey and I had that talk, his younger brother Graham walked into his mother's house stoned.

"I'm going to bed," he said. "Good night." Graham then hurried his way through the kitchen and started up the stairs. He had been with some friends, and I had come to his mother's to pick up some of my mail that was still being delivered there.

"Graham?" I said. "You're home early. Everything okay?"

He was still in motion and nearly to the top of the steps when he said, "Yep, all good. Good night."

Graham never voluntarily came home early from anywhere, never just rushed past his mother or me without something to say. Graham was a talker.

"Whoa. Hold on. What's going on?"

"Just tired, Dad. See ya," he said from the top step.

"Graham, come on down here."

"Seriously, Dad. I'm really tired," he said, looking over the railing from the upstairs landing to the room below.

"Graham?"

I could see his eyes now—wide open and red, darting corner to corner.

"Dad," Graham said, hesitantly, "I'm a little freaked." He walked swiftly down the steps and into the family room, speaking with the quickness of a rapper. "I just had a *little*. Really. Someone had some stuff. I was just curious. But it's got me all, I don't know…wired-up."

When Graham was a toddler, his grandfather snuck him on a ride at a church carnival. There was a horizontal line drawn across the ride's entranceway door: *You Must be THIS Big to Ride This Ride.* Graham's Pappy ignored it, and the fat man with the ponytail taking tickets ignored Graham's size. Graham and his grandfather got inside one of the four round cars with the clowns painted on the side. Their bodies tossed and turned as the car spun and twisted, and the floor rose and fell. The look on Graham's face that night was the same as it was this night—eyes wide open and red, darting corner to corner.

"Be honest with me," I said.

"One of the guys had weed. That's it," he whispered as if telling his sins to a priest in a church confessional.

"You smoked it?"

"Yeah, but I don't know why I feel like this," Graham said, his hands shaking as he ran them through his hair.

"You've done this before?"

"Yeah," he said apologetically. "But Dad, this is way weird."

"What do you know about what you smoked? Who gave it to you? Be honest, with me."

"I *am* being honest," he said, now pacing back and forth along an imaginary five-foot line. "I feel like there's stuff running under my skin. My head is spinning." He nervously rubbed his arms and then his thighs. "It doesn't seem normal. Is this normal?"

Graham could distort the facts with the best of the teenagers, but when he was ready to tell the truth, he revealed it with a raw and open heart, no hesitation, details gushing like summer water from a city fire hydrant. I walked Graham to the sofa, told him to sit, close his eyes, and try to relax.

We sat and talked for nearly an hour. Not only about what happened earlier that night—how a friend of a friend came to the party with the dope, how the boys snuck outside in the back yard to smoke it, and how the smoke burned on their throats—but also about the new Batman movie and if the Steelers would make the playoffs this year. We talked about drugs, dope, and the friends who were using. We talked about girls and school. We talked until he was calm, soothed enough to sleep. And the next day, he and his mother talked, and he and I talked again. To this day I'm still not sure if Graham's reaction that night was because he got caught, because he had some unusual physical reaction to the weed, or if there was something else in those joints. And I'm not sure if Graham kept his promise, but that night he swore he would never smoke again.

One year later my thirty-year-old cousin died of a heroin overdose. Police found him slumped over the wheel of his car in the parking lot of a housing project where drugs were sold like lemon ice on a hot summer day. The needle was still in his arm. Sean had grown up watching his father drink himself into a permanent state of confusion. Sean was eight years old when he began trying to alter his reality in one way or another— beer, bourbon, Southern Comfort, weed, pills, cocaine. He was kicked out of college and lost job after job, including work as an emergency medical technician because he was accused of stealing the medication from the ambulances. He was in and out of rehab for years. Months before he died, Sean apparently had cleaned up again, and this time there seemed to be a bit more hope. It certainly wasn't the first time he tried to go straight. In his early twenties, after returning home from a month-long, head-clearing road trip, he dedicated himself to getting healthy. He was eating well, exercising, even writing poetry. It worked for a time, but it was difficult to tell if it was genuine, especially to those who had closely witnessed his behavior before. However, in the weeks before he died, Sean was talking openly for the first time about how his addictions had ruined opportunities, destroyed friendships, and fractured his family. He appeared more clearly aware of what drugs had done to him and how he might be able to live without them. He was smiling more, laughing more, and had found new work as a caddy at Oakmont Country Club outside Pittsburgh. He loved walking the green grass, hearing the birds, and giving golf tips to members and guests. And he was getting good at the job. So good, he was preparing to work for one of the professionals who would qualify to play in the U.S. Open Championship at Oakmont in the summer of 2007.

When I told Casey how Sean had died, he wanted to know why no one had noticed any of the signs Sean was using again. He wondered whether Sean's addictions were genetic, considering the alcoholic life of Sean's father. Casey wanted simply to understand. But Graham was different. Understanding Sean's demons appeared less important, even meaningless. When I told Graham the news that Sean had died, he didn't say a word or ask a single question. Instead, he cried as hard as I can ever remember him crying.

We exhausted our three days in Denver, hitting *On the Road* landmarks and Beat Generation haunts. We even tried to find the home Kerouac once owned in the city's Lakewood (once called Westwood) neighborhood, but we were uncertain of the exact house. The address didn't quite match up. Through it all, the boys appeared to be enjoying themselves. Graham got a kick riding in Brad's open-roof Jeep and Casey captured most everything on his cameras.

"Can't wait to get to San Francisco!" Brad yelled from behind the wheel of the RV as we made our way down the street in front of his apartment.

We left Denver at dawn, coffee mugs in hand.

Chapter 7
The Color and the Noise

I was surprised it had taken almost one thousand miles before we first argued about music. A road trip needs tunes, and I had made several playlists on my iPhone, loading it up with Dylan, Beatles, CSN&Y, Lucinda Williams, Pearl Jam, Miles Davis. Brad was into it. Graham was not.

"I know I can plug my headphones in and listen to my own stuff. But Dad, can we put something else on in here? Seriously."

We were nearing Grand Junction when the debate began to ramp-up.

"Come on guys, you know you like your Dad's music," Brad said, gesturing with one hand and the other on the steering wheel. "It's the only stuff that endures, man!"

"But it's the same thing, over and over. Help me!" said Casey, taking his eyes away from the work of downloading video to his laptop.

I liked to think I embraced a good bit of new music, but it just wasn't the boys' music, and it especially wasn't Graham's. During Graham's early high school years, music was everything to him. It represented a large part of his life. He listened to his iPod continuously, took up the drums, and was desperate to start a band with his guitar-playing friends. Although the music of *On the Road* was jazz, I was certain Graham would see the similarities between his love of rock and the music that liberated the book's characters, the freedom both kinds of music represented, the rebellion. In the final months of his freshman year, music was all that was getting through to Graham. He was failing his classes, and there appeared to be scant chance he would find a way to squeak out some Ds. The possibilities were slipping away.

"Forget it," his counselor said. "You're wasting energy. It's best to write this off."

Graham had seen as many as five counselors since seventh grade. We even tried an art therapist who searched for answers with paint, crayons, and Elmer's glue. But things progressively worsened. It's not that he was a problem kid—getting into trouble, anti-social, or violent. He was exactly the opposite— thoughtful, considerate, gentle. Teachers liked Graham. Even the janitor at his elementary school thought he was "an absolute joy."

"He's a great kid," he told me during a scheduled parents' reception at the school as he walked the hall emptying garbage cans. "So articulate, well-spoken."

Parents in the neighborhood thought highly of him, too.

"Do you know what Graham did?" one mother told me. "My kids were getting picked on, and he stood up for them." She had triplets—boys, small for their age, scrawny, even delicate, and three grades behind Graham in elementary school. On the walk home after the final bell, a fifth-grader with a crew cut and the build of a dump truck tried to corner the triplets near the back of the school, telling them he was going to "kick their asses." Graham stepped in, his hands on his hips, his wide shoulders filling the space between the boys and the bully.

"You're going to have to kick mine first," Graham said.

The bully backed off.

The paradox over Graham's grades began in the last year of elementary school and like an insidious infection, spread to his middle and then high school classes where his grade percentages took a dive so deep that his mother and I were already pulling together the paperwork for summer school and the five-year high school plan. Graham couldn't see the link between doing homework and passing. He shined on tests, but homework was lost, forgotten, or willingly dismissed. That put him in a bad place. And Graham didn't seem to care.

There were other concerns. He'd been caught disregarding the truth, telling his mother and me he had done things and been places he hadn't. And he'd snatched money out of his mother's purse to pay off debts to friends at school. His confessions revealed he had been buying Gatorade from the school's vending machine and extra food in the cafeteria— daily hotdogs, hamburgers, and pizza. He was already a big kid, standing nearly six feet and weighing 250, and now he was getting bigger. There had been discussions with therapists about eating disorders and early trauma in his younger years. When Graham was a toddler there had been a burglary at our home and it had shaken him, creating a nighttime nervousness. He struggled through the cancer deaths of his maternal grandmother and his paternal grandfather, and doctors thought he might be somehow soothing the trauma through eating.

Frankly, the doctors, his counselors, his teachers, and his parents were all guessing. None of us really knew what to do for Graham.

I started to refer to all of Graham's troubles as the *noise* in his head. It was the random racket, the crackling of the misplaced and misdirected electrical impulses, the dissonant symphonic sounds of a drunken wind orchestra. The *noise* was drowning out all the soul's quiet conversations, the soothing words of a mind trying to talk itself into balance. But all around the turbulence, there was color, a dense pigment. Graham was not gray, beige, green, or yellow. Graham was purple—the combination of red hot and cool blue. Not the delicate lighter shades of lavender, but the deeper, more complicated hues of the crocus, the favorite color of Cleopatra, the color of robes worn by royalty and men of spiritual high rank, the color of the military medal given to those wounded in battle, the color of Jimi Hendrix's musical haze. The intricate combination of the color and the noise formed the center of Graham's complexity, a labyrinth no one had yet to navigate.

Still, the simple part of the puzzle was that Graham was a likeable guy—energetic, social, and witty, with sharp intellect and passion, especially for music.

"Who's singing this song?" I'd ask him when the two of us where alone in my car, the iPod playing through the car speakers loud enough to vibrate the seats.

"Hello, Dad," he'd yell through the music, as if I had asked the most moronic question. "It's Robert Plant. Led Zeppelin. Hello."

The answers were usually Bob Dylan, John Lennon, The Kinks, Joni Mitchell, Cream, Neil Young, or someone more obscure like Steve Earle, Richard Thompson, or Patty Griffin. I would even throw a Charlie Parker in there now and then. Most of the time, Graham knew the artists and I would be smug, knowing I had taught him a thing or two about great talent.

There were times he tested me.

"Who is this, Dad?" he'd say, certain I had no clue.

"I think I've heard this before…uh…is it Slipfoot?"

"Geez, Dad," he'd say, laughing. "It's Slip*knot.*"

Graham loved Heavy Metal. Although the music selection on his iPod was quite eclectic, he played Metal almost exclusively. Along with Slipknot, and Lamb of God, and other "Metal Gods" as he called them, he listened to Johnny Cash, and Frank Sinatra, and even Boston, the pop band from the '70s. But there's no doubt, Metal was his favorite. He even presented in his high school speech class on the history of Metal music. That's where I learned about the different strains—Heavy Metal, Death Metal, Doom Metal, Stoner Metal, Speed Metal, Castle Metal, and Thrash Metal. Who knew?

A couple of years ago, I took Graham and his brother to a Crosby, Stills, and Nash concert. It was the boys' first rock concert, and I thought it was a pretty safe introduction. But now at the age of fifteen, Graham wanted to attend a concert that featured *his* music. He asked repeatedly.

"Dad, Atreyu is playing in the city. Can I go?"

"Don't think so. Grades are too bad. Sorry."

"Dad, Children of Bodom is playing in Milwaukee, only three hours away. What about it?"

"You're still not on track. Plus, you're not going to a Metal concert without some supervision."

David W. Berner

That was the opening he needed. *Supervision.*

"So, you would let me go to a concert, but only if you came with me? Is that it?" He asked this with the anticipation of a kid who was just told he could open a Christmas present in July.

I began to believe it might be good to get Graham away from all that was troubling him, just for a little while. He needed to be in a place that would thrill him, a place where he wouldn't have his parents and his teachers continually riding him. Of course, I didn't tell him I was thinking this way. I wasn't about to open *that* door, just yet.

"There is a concert coming up at the end of the summer. It's huge. It's like, six bands, and it's at the outdoor theater down in the south suburbs somewhere. Slipknot is one of the bands." His big blue eyes grew softer, and he tilted his head to one side, looking innocent, so young.

"Take a look at the date, check the ticket prices, see what's available, and see if you can get some friends to go along. I'll think about it. Not promising *anything.*"

I knew if the price wasn't outrageous, I was going to say yes. But, I truly did not understand what it would be like at a daylong, brain-bashing, outdoor Metal concert with four teenage boys.

First stop on the day of the concert was lunch at White Castle. The infamous burgers are about three-inches square with warm, mushy buns, overcooked beef, and a pinch of onions thrown in the mix to give them a hint of flavor they otherwise wouldn't have. I quit counting the number of tiny burgers consumed by Graham and his three friends at somewhere around forty.

"I'm keeping this," Graham said, holding up the cardboard box that once held all those burgers. "It's a souvenir."

The outside amphitheater sat in the middle of a large field with a few scattered homes nearby and a golf course a couple of miles away. We arrived two hours before the first band was to take the stage, and the parking lot was already filling up.

"Does that guy have a swastika tattooed on the back of his head?" I said to no one in particular.

"Yeah, he does," said Jack, one of Graham's friends. "That's freakin' sick."

"Some of these people are wacky. It's just the way it is," Graham said, seemingly knowing what to expect and in many ways already accepting what he would witness.

I concluded early on that most Metal concertgoers are people on the fringes. I always wondered where the girl with twelve piercings on her face, blue hair, and both legs covered in tattoos gets a job. But that's what a parent thinks, right? This was not a place for parents or for thinking.

But I was also surprised to see what some would call *normal* people standing in line at the entrance gate.

"Dad, are those our neighbors?" Graham asked, pointing toward a couple at the south end of the gate. They looked like they were in their early thirties. Both wore Levi jeans. He was in a polo shirt, and she wore what appeared to be a DKNY blouse. There were no visible piercings or tattoos. They looked like they were heading for COSTCO to shop for giant containers of ketchup and pickles.

"No, not our neighbors. Looks like them, though," I said.

"Does that guy have a stud through the back of his neck?" Graham's friend Corey asked.

The teenager was shirtless with a shaved head, black jeans, and sandals.

"Yep, it's a stud. Straight through the neck," Graham said matter-of-factly.

Graham didn't seem phased by any of the spectacle, and I shouldn't have been surprised. I had seen plenty of students at Graham's high school with all kinds of body art. Although I wasn't sure any of that art was anything quite like what we were witnessing.

"Dad, you're not weirded out about this, are you?" Graham asked.

"Bud, remember, I teach college, I see a lot of wacky clothes and styles. I'm good, really." I lied. I was just a *little* weirded out.

The music was loud, but no louder than concerts I remembered attending in my twenties. Still, listening to this music was a workout. After each musical set, it was as if you had just finished a run at the gym. It was the driving force of the music, the intensity and relentless throbbing set it apart from any concert I had been to before. And the lyrics? I wasn't completely prepared for them either. There were plenty of "fucks" and "kills" and "hates." But to be fair, "love" was also in the mix. Even "pray" came up a few times. And the names of the bands—Disturbed, Mastodon, Dragonforce, and of course, Slipknot—were all familiar to me because of Graham's iPod playlist.

"What do you think?" Graham asked between the first and second band of the day.

"You know, Graham, I'm enjoying this," I said, surprising myself with the answer. "Not exactly my type of music, but this is doable."

Graham laughed.

"Wait until you see Disturbed, then Slipknot. Oh my God." Graham put his arm around my shoulder and looked me straight in the eyes. "I don't want you to be scared, okay?" This was the Graham I knew. This was the boy who cared, had passion, and desperately wanted me to accept his music. "These guys are good musicians, Dad, they're just a little…nuts. Hang in there."

All Graham needed to know was that Dad was on his side.

"Graham, I wouldn't be here if I didn't want to be," I said. He smiled.

"Can we get something to eat?" Graham asked.

"Here's twenty bucks," I said, handing him the cash I had stuffed in the front pocket of my jeans. "No corndogs, no funnel cakes, okay?"

"Yeah, yeah. Got it," he said, jumping up and crawling over the seats in front of us, his buddies right there with him.

I sat alone in the stands, watching the roadies take down band equipment and replace it with more. I could also see Graham and his friends walk through the aisles and out to the food court, laughing and knocking into each other the way teenage boys do to show affection. One of them eyed a pretty girl. She appeared to be around eighteen with shoulder-length blonde hair, wearing jean shorts and a Metallica tee-shirt. One of his friends tapped Graham on the shoulder and all four of them stopped in their steps to watch her walk. Music, friends, girls—what more could four teenage boys want?

The last two bands scheduled to take the stage were Graham's favorites, and the anticipation for one of them—Slipknot—was overflowing.

"They wear these masks, never show their faces, and you know the masks are going to be *insane*," Graham said, excitedly sharing a little insight into his favorite musicians.

Some fans came to the concert wearing Slipknot masks. "Each one somehow symbolizes the stages of the band's life," Graham explained. To me, the fans wearing the masks looked like characters from one of the string of Halloween horror movies. "And you know, Joey Jordison is going to be in chains, or something wacky." Jordison was the band's drummer, one of Graham's musical heroes.

Disturbed played next. And if I had to pick a favorite band of the night, this was it. The music was hard and powerful, but the lyrics, although dark and frequently raw, were deeper and more complex than the other bands.

"That song, 'Prayer.' That's pretty good, Graham. The singer must have some real pain to work through," I said in the relative calm between the end of the Disturbed set and the beginning of Slipknot's.

"Know what it's about?" Graham asked me. "The singer's sister committed suicide, and he reached out to God, sort of became religious and wrote a song about it. It was his way of getting over her death."

"How do you know this, Graham?"

"I read," he said with a smirk.

This sounded familiar. When I was his age, I devoured *Rolling Stone* magazine, consuming every article about my favorite singers and bands. Did you know that Dylan's "It Ain't Me Babe" is about Joan Baez? Did you know that CSN&Y's "Our House" is Graham Nash's love song to Joni Mitchell? Did you know that the Beatles' "Blackbird" is Paul McCartney's answer to the civil rights movement? I had suitcases full of this kind of stuff. Graham did, too.

Slipknot finally came to the stage. And each band member was in costume, wearing those masks and wielding big attitude.

"Fuck YOU," the lead singer screamed into the microphone. The crowd yelled back its own greeting. "Fuck YOU, TOO." It was a Metal thing, I guess.

Slipknot burst into its first song with the force of a bulldozer, the wall of sound smacking against my face, rattling my cheekbones.

Graham and his friends went directly into head-banging mode, stiffening their necks and twirling their hair in circles. Graham's locks were long enough to hit me in the ear.

The boys and the rest of the crowd were now on their feet, pumping fists in the air and belting out song lyrics that I could neither understand nor hear over the sledgehammer guitars and drums. I stood along with everyone else, but my eyes were not on the stage, they were on Graham. He was jumping to the beat of the music, his body moving to involuntary impulses, his hair still swirling, his eyes fixed on his musical heroes.

David W. Berner

"Graham!" I yelled, trying to overcome the massive sound. He didn't respond.

"Graham!" I screamed, grabbing his elbow. "This is what you needed, isn't it?"

Graham couldn't hear me through the dense and rhythmic thump that surrounded us. It didn't matter. Like Kerouac in the presence of Charlie Parker or Thelonious Monk, Graham was before his heroes; the "prophets" leading the stray back "to the golden world that Jesus came from." All the work we had to do as father and son would be hard, tedious, taxing, difficult, disappointing, frustrating—but it had all vanished temporarily that afternoon in the sharing of this mad music.

Chapter 8
Ukulele

We were making our way through Colorado, and anticipated a steady pace through Utah until we were somewhere on the western border, close to Provo. The boys settled in for a lengthy stretch of driving. Casey slept on the big queen bed in the rear of the RV, and Graham pulled up a movie on the computer. Brad and I took the time to catch up.

"So you're serious about the culinary school?" I asked.

"Well, I love food, been cooking for years. I love wine. I ran a restaurant. Seems a good idea," Brad said, hesitating for a moment. "I think."

"Okay, which is it?"

"Fuck, I don't know. It sounds like a good idea. Lot of money, though. But I do get to go to Italy."

"Got to do what you love."

"That's what they say. I'm just not sure what the fuck that is."

I knew exactly what he was talking about. I'd been there. After struggling to find an exit from daily journalism, a monotonous grind, I finally thought I had begun to create my place in the world. Following my divorce, I went back to school, got my MA in Education and Teaching, taught eighth grade literature in a rough-and-tumble school in a Chicago suburb, then secured a job teaching college. I was happy again. The divorce was difficult, amicable but heartbreaking. Then, my father died.

"I have just had one hell of a year," said Brad. "Another fucking divorce, sold my business, and then my dad dies. Jesus, I just want to *drink*." Brad joked a lot about soothing himself with bottles of wine after his first marriage broke up. And yes, he did his share of that. So did I. Easy to do when your world flips upside down. It was never a serious problem, just a temporary bridge over rough waters.

"Well, maybe this trip is going to give you some...*clarity*," I said, laughing. It was our take on Sal Paradise's search for "*it*." We had been throwing around that word—*clarity*—since we first started surveying maps for this journey. The road will give us *clarity*. The wide-open spaces will give us *clarity*. Kerouac will give us *clarity*. It became a running gag.

"Oh well, shit," Brad said. "No clarity yet!"

I guess I didn't have clarity either. I was still working through the emotional potholes of my divorce and the death of my father. There wasn't a day, sometimes an hour, when he didn't pop into my mind, show up unexpectedly, or was tossed in by outside forces.

And I interrupted my conversation with Brad because Dad was right there again, poking at my brain.

"Dad used to love this song," I said. "Boys, remember how Pappy used to sing this?"

Playing through my iPod and into the RV was "Desperado," the old Eagles song. When I was younger, I would sing and play it on the piano, and Dad would tear up. Something about the loneliness, the longing for love, touched my father. I never asked why the song put him in a melancholy mood.

Dad was a music man. Not because he could play an instrument with any virtuosity, but because he simply loved it. Although "Desperado" evoked a sadness in him, he found joy in so many other songs; delight poured out of him when he heard his favorites. It was not the kind of pleasure a man experiences when he listens to opera and permits the soaring aria to bring him to tears, or when a skilled pianist strikes the notes in the tender melody of a Beethoven piano sonata and allows his senses to overflow. For Dad, the musical emotions came less from the heart of a cultured man and more from the gut of a workingman. Merle Haggard and Johnny Cash were favorites. He loved the playfulness of a honky-tonk keyboard, the twang of a Nashville guitar, and the sassy, tough-guy smokiness of Sinatra's "My Kind of Town. "

Still, what my father really wanted to do was to play an instrument well enough to be called a musician. He'd listen to the big Magnavox console hi-fi stereo in our home, point to the speakers, and say, "I want to be able to do *that.*" *That* was many times the twinkling of piano keys or the strum of a banjo.

Dad wasn't completely void of musical ability. He could knock out a pretty solid version of "Chopsticks" on the piano, and he knew a one-handed, ten-note ragtime lick. He could also blow a little Chicago-style harmonica, playing the same simple blues notes over and over. But his best amateur performance came from an unlikely instrument: a four-string ukulele. It was a beat-up, dark brown, soprano version, the smallest kind made. I don't know how Dad came to own the ukulele. Maybe someone gave it to him. Maybe he bought it. But the uke, as he called it, was always within arm's reach. It could be found leaning against the wall in the living room next to Dad's chair just in case he had the urge to play the one and only song he could perform with absolute pride.

"*Five foot two, eyes of blue.*" Dad would belt out the words, while his left hand contorted into position to play simple chords on the ukulele's tiny frets, and his right skipped a felt pick in a blurry rat-a-tat across the nylon strings.

"*But, oh, what those five foot can do!*" Dad's head would bob to the beat as his eyes concentrated on the ukulele's frets, making certain he played the right notes at exactly the right time.

"*Has anybody seen my gal?*" When he'd finish a verse, Dad would speed-strum through a three-chord progression, creating a carnival-like sound.

I'm not sure how "Has Anybody Seen My Gal?" became the quintessential ukulele song. Maybe it had the perfect melody for the instrument, enough razzmatazz in the lyrics to produce a smile from just about anyone, including a big one from Dad.

"*Turned up nose, turned down hose, never had no other beaus.*"

Each time, Dad would play the tune flawlessly, giving the last chord a thwack-thwack-thwackity-thwack for a song-and-dance-man finish.

Before playing the song though, Dad would always take a few minutes to tune the ukulele. "Besides *Gal*, 'Tuning' is the only other song I know," he'd joke.

"My dog has fleas. My…dog…has…fleas." It was the phrase Dad would sing as he plucked the strings. There was something about the tenor of those words that helped to tune the ukulele. *"My…dog…has…fleas. My dog has…fleas."* He'd hold out the last word—*fleeeeeas*—as he'd twist the key to stretch the final string.

It was a particularly aggressive form of prostate cancer that weakened my father, and eventually forced him into a hospital bed in my parents' bedroom and placed in home hospice care. Before long, Dad became too weak to play the ukulele, and the instrument fell silent.

Late one night, one of the many in the final months of waiting for Dad to die, I sat alone in my father's chair and lifted the ukulele to my knee. Years before, I had learned to play the guitar and had fooled around a little with the ukulele. I wiped the dust from the frets, put my thumb to the strings, and thought about all the songs Dad loved so much—the country tunes, the Sinatra standards, and of course that one classic ukulele song. But there was only one song my limited ability could muster.

"My…dog…has…fleas." I sang the line softly, picking each string and turning each key, hoping to find the perfect note. *"My…dog…dog has…my…dog."* I plucked the strings over and over, making tonal adjustments the best I knew how. *"My…my dog…dog…dog."* But I was having a hard time. The sounds were somehow…*off*…and the pitch of each string was unsteady. Still, I was determined to produce that familiar, sweet twang my father once created.

As the long night sank into its deepest hours, I kept at it, singing and humming each note, plucking each string. And somewhere in the early morning hours, my fingers grew tired, my eyes lost their battle with heavy lids, and I fell asleep with my chin on my chest and the ukulele in my lap.

Another one of those big green highway signs stood before us: Moab 55 miles.

"Dad, can I talk to you about something?" Casey made his way between the seats in the cab. "Are we gonna stop anywhere?"

"Well, I think we need to keep truckin'," I said, believing we must get to the RV park before dark.

"We're only a few miles from Moab. It's just a bit off the highway. It's supposed to be pretty cool," Casey said. "We aren't going to just keep driving all the time, are we?"

I looked at Brad.

"It'll get us to the Provo area pretty late at night. What do you think?" I asked.

"Well, we're here. Go for it," Brad said. "Right, Case?"

Casey smiled.

Moab looked like Mars, colossal red rock formations from outer space. Towering rocks with ancient holes worn through the middle, the work of a prehistoric river. Massive, long narrow boulders, the size of city buildings, seemingly balancing on the edges of others just like them. Rock arches stretching from one immense cropping to another, as if God's architect was experimenting. We spent several hours driving and hiking in Moab, each of us admitting it was a saintly place, unworldly, soulful.

I thanked Casey for insisting we break from our planned route. It was a precedent we needed to set early in the trip. Some of Casey's best photographs came from our time in Moab, but it wasn't just the digital memories from this mystical land that remained. Electrical synapses ignited among the four of us in Utah like some sort of new age ritual, bonding this group of travelers for the first time. We drove up State Route 191 and left Moab as the sun was setting, silently saying our final prayers in a holy place.

It was nearly two hundred miles to Provo and the RV park where we had a reservation for the night. That meant three hours of driving in the dark.

"Let's stay in a hotel tonight, guys," I said from the passenger seat.

"We could use a good bed, don't you think?" said Brad, from behind the wheel.

I phoned the office at the RV park and cancelled our reservation, figuring we'd find a vacant room somewhere along the highway.

Casey napped on the seat just behind the cab, and Graham lay his head on the small table in the kitchen area. You could hear his snoring. And Brad and I settled in on the road with cups of coffee and John Coltrane on the stereo.

David W. Berner

"You were talking about your dad and his music," said Brad. "Dad ever tell you to turn that shit down?"

"My dad tolerated a lot," I said, laughing. "Steppenwolf blaring from my record player. Do you remember that drum solo in 'In-A-Gadda-Da-Vida'?"

"Hell yeah."

"I played Zeppelin and The Who loud and long. He never said a thing. Then when I started playing in a rock band with a bunch of high school buddies, and we'd practice in our basement, Dad would come down and listen. He'd sit on the cellar steps and tap his feet, big smile on his face."

"Oh, not my dad. But he did like his music," Brad said softly. After a moment, he sighed, trying to exhale a memory. I lightly tapped my fist on his shoulder, gave Coltrane a little volume, and turned to look out the passenger window into the black Utah night.

Chapter 9
Ghost Boxing

It was just before midnight. We were motoring west somewhere in the Wasatch or Oquirrh range of Utah east of Provo when I broke the silence.

"Is that coming right our way?" It was a tersely delivered question on a desperately dark high-elevation road. We had been weaving and bobbing through the steep, rugged hills, when from the passenger seat I could see a single light in the distance. It was aiming directly at us.

"What the hell is that?" Brad said from the driver's seat, nervously laughing, the way one does when there's a rush of adrenaline, a sense of imminent danger.

"I really hope that thing turns or moves somewhere," I said, tightening my grip on the door handle, my eyes locking on the slowly enlarging light.

"What's going on?" Graham said, awakening from the bunk above the cab and peering down between Brad and me.

Casey pulled the headphones from his ears. "Something up?" he asked.

"The light. You see that?" I said.

"Looks like it's coming dead on," said Graham.

"What do you think it is?" said Casey, reaching for his video camera and placing it against his eye.

"Better not be a damn car," said Brad. "Jesus!"

Driving to this point had been relatively uneventful. When Brad took the RV through the Colorado Rockies, it was a bit of a nervous passage for those of us not used to the dramatic rise and fall of the mountains. I asked Brad to slow down to help ease my anxiety, but he was like Dean Moriarty—confident, a god behind the wheel. All in all, the RV ran smoothly on the highways and handled well through traffic. However, this was different. It was late at night and *dark as the inside of your hat*—something my father used to say. We were tired, hungry, and irritated by how slowly the miles seemed to be ticking off through Utah, as if the state's mileage meter had miscalculated the distances from one point to another. And now this mysterious, threatening light.

Then we all heard it, a faint but growing sound, a chug, a metronomic click and clang.

"It's a damn train!" I cried out.

We had been watching the single headlight of a locomotive, running on tracks exactly parallel to the right side of the road. In the dark distance it appeared to be using us as a target.

Casey captured the train and our collective uneasiness through the lens of his camera. He had been taking photos and video all along the trip, but this was one of the first times he'd reached for the camera with personal eagerness.

"This is really your trip, Dad. I get that," Casey said, a few minutes after the train scare. "And I'll record all the Kerouac stuff you want, but I want to make it my trip too, so I've got to take other shots. And that mountain train, well, *that* was one little freaky moment, especially watching it with one eye closed."

The road trip was no longer mine; it was ours.

There had been a massive power outage outside Provo, and residents snatched up nearly all the once vacant rooms, hoping for better places to sleep until the electricity was back. We stopped at nearly every La Quinta, Motel 6, and Clarion off the highway exits.

"Driving this damn thing in these parking lots is a bitch," Brad said, attempting to maneuver the RV out of the way of parked cars and driving lanes.

"They've got nothing," I said, walking from our fifth stop at a motel desk and toward the cab's open window. "They say there's a Sheraton or something down the road about twenty miles, but they only have one room and it's smoking."

It was nearly 2:00 a.m. before we found a place for the night. We slept until checkout.

Somewhere in one of Kerouac's hundreds of notebooks, little spiral-bound tablets he'd tuck away in his pocket, he first wrote about the plot for *On the Road*. He summarized it by describing it as a story about two guys hitchhiking to California in search of something they don't really find, losing themselves on the road, and coming back hopeful of something else. It was late morning, and I was sitting alone on a bench just outside the motel's front door waiting for the others when I thought about Kerouac's pencil-scribbled idea for a book. The storyline was at the heart of every road trip. The one taken by the newly graduated high school kid in the months before heading off to college, the university student at spring break, or the family off on the quintessentially American summer vacation. When I was just a kid, Dad packed his new green 1960 Chevy Impala with bathing suits and shorts, put my mother and me in the front bench seat, his mother, mother-in-law, and my great-aunt in the back, and took off from Pittsburgh to Port St. Lucie, Florida, to visit the home of his Aunt Florence. Years later, my mother told me they really hadn't made much of a plan, driving down the highway in the heat of summer with just a road map on the dashboard and two weeks to kill. It might have seemed to many like an innocent summer road trip, but it was more than that, I think. My father had never been that far from home, even when he was in the U.S. Army, he was stationed in Maryland, just a five-hour drive away. His honeymoon was in Erie, Pennsylvania, at a cheap motel by the lake, and he may have made a day trip once or twice to Niagara Falls. But that was about it. So, you might say, the drive to Florida was his Kerouac trip, his best chance to go out and lose himself on the road and come home with a renewed sense of life and who he was. And like me, he was a father who couldn't imagine not bringing along the ones he loved, especially his five-year-old son.

That family trip was certainly on a different scale, but I could relate to what my father must have been thinking along the way. I had made a few road trips as a young man, right around the same age as Dad at the time of the Florida vacation, but not much more than four-to-five hour drives from home. Getaways to the in-laws' cottage in Upstate New York, Caribbean beaches, and golf in Scotland with a side trip to Paris came when I was an adult, a married man with kids. But I knew that road trips could be a glue for friends, family, relationships. And so, when my divorce came, and I desperately wanted to make new memories, new connections with my young sons, travel was sometimes the antidote.

Most of the United Airlines gates at Chicago's O'Hare Airport on a weekday before noon are busy enough to fill all the seats with waiting passengers, forcing the remaining travelers to sit on the floor. But the boys and I were headed for Eugene, Oregon, and it wasn't a popular destination that day, if it ever is. So the boys and I sank into chairs and rested our carry-ons in the empty seats beside us. McDonald's bags had been flattened onto the boys' laps, small makeshift trays to hold their hamburgers and fries. It was close enough to noon for McDonald's and there was still enough morning for me to sip a tall coffee-of-the-day from one of the three Starbucks in Terminal One. We were comfortable, unhurried. Not the typical experience at one of the world's busiest airports. And that's probably why I was able to spot him, not lose him in the customary airport mob, and look him directly in the eyes.

"Boys!" I said, jumping to my feet, instinctively thinking I could get a better look. "It's…it's…"

Graham, holding a fry in one hand and chewing another,

was first to lift his head from his food. "What?"

"That's Ali. It's Muhammad Ali."

Ali sat on the back of a small, flat trailer connected to a golf-cart driven by an airport worker. It was one of those vehicles you often see carrying luggage through the terminals. Ali held a brown satchel, and wore a dark gray suit and a blue tie. His face was expressionless until his eyes caught mine. It was only an instant. If it had been anyone else it would have been a fleeting, forgettable moment. But this was Muhammad Ali. When he smiled at me, it was if as he had known me my entire life.

"He winked," I said to no one in particular. Then I turned toward the boys. "He smiled and winked at me."

Casey was up from his seat and standing beside me.

"Yeah, I've seen him," he said as we both watched the trailer weave its way slowly down the terminal's hall. "He's the boxer, right?"

The boys were twelve and ten years old, and Ali was a name they'd heard before, a face they'd seen on TV, but not a person who resonated with their lives. At this stage the boys couldn't get enough of James Bond movies and the Cubs' Sammy Sosa. To them Ali was the guy Will Smith played in a movie, an old fighter, a man suffering from some sort of disease.

"He winked because he knew," I said, watching the airport vehicle and Ali disappear into the terminal crowd. "He knew that I knew who he was."

"Isn't he sick?" Graham said. "Doesn't he shake or something?"

"How did you know that?" I asked.

"Something on ESPN, I think." Graham loved football. Played it, watched it, talked about it. ESPN was a favorite channel.

"He has Parkinson's," I said. "It messes up the nervous system."

"Can he talk?" Casey asked.

"He can. But it's labored. I think he has a very difficult time of it."

"Wasn't he, like, the greatest boxer ever?" asked Graham.

"Yep. Float like a butterfly, sting like a bee."

"What?"

The boys had never heard Ali's most memorable words.

My work as a journalist had allowed me to meet a lot of prominent people. I had interviewed Jimmy Carter, Ted Kennedy, Bill Gates, and countless others about their lives, their work, their fame. I've been rarely star-struck. But in an interview, there's a protocol, an assumed dance by the journalist and the celebrated. It's usually a planned event, your roles are clear, and many times you take from an interview just about what you had anticipated. But it's the unexpected meeting, the unforeseen sighting that burns an imprint on your memory. And many times that comes outside the reporter's life, outside the job, leaving behind a remarkable moment that forever resurfaces and demands to be retold. I saw William Kennedy Smith, the nephew of JFK and RFK and Ted, at Chicago's Coco Pazzo restaurant. He was eating ravioli with a beautiful young woman. There was the time I saw James Garner peeing at the urinal in the men's room of the Gandy Dancer tavern in Pittsburgh, and Oprah getting into a black limo near the big GAP store on Chicago's Michigan Avenue.

"Cool that we saw him, Dad," Casey said, sitting back down to what was left of his early lunch.

"Yep, quite cool," I said, still standing, my eyes bouncing between the boys and the long terminal hallway. I was hoping my sons might get the same kick out of this brief chance sighting as I did, but it could never be the same for them. "Guys," I asked. "Is there anyone you would really like to meet? Someone really important?" Ali didn't give them the thrill he gave me, but I still hoped they would someday experience that electric moment when you're in the presence of someone special, historic, legendary. Not the giddiness of hero-worship fueled by the cult of celebrity, but the more meaningful realization that there are people in the world who have made a difference, and if you are lucky enough to walk next to them, figuratively or literally, even for a few seconds, you should savor it. Idealistic thinking? Maybe. But it was what I wanted for my sons.

Graham finished the last bite of his hamburger and slurped down the final straw-full of his diet Coke.

"Does this place have a pool?" asked Graham, forgetting about Ali and ignoring the question I asked about meeting someone important.

"What?"

"A pool?"

"The place we're going?"

"Yeah, the resort in, what is it? Brandon or something?"

"*Bandon*. Bandon, Oregon," I said. The Ali moment had vanished, and now Graham was far more interested in the possibility of jumping from a diving board into the deep end.

"No pool. Sorry, but there's dune buggy riding on the big sand dunes near the ocean."

The place in Bandon was an understated golf resort, revered by those who played the game, but virtually unknown to the average vacationer. The owners asked me to come out and play the courses, review and write about the facility for a golf publication. Bringing the boys along seemed a good idea. It had only been a few months since my divorce from their mother, and this was a little vacation that wouldn't exhaust my still rocky-from-the-breakup bank account. More importantly, this was *my* trip with the boys, the first getaway with them since I moved out of the house, and the first since my father's death. I was still laboring through the pain of both, and often thinking about how heartbroken my father was when he learned my marriage was ending and our family would be splintered. Dad was all too familiar with a boy's life without a father. And although I was sure he was certain I would never be the kind of absent man his father was, Dad's childhood had undoubtedly scarred him enough that those smothered emotions could be re-ignited. The end of my marriage was one of those times. I had packed one suitcase for the Oregon trip, but I was carrying plenty of other baggage.

"What else is there to do?" Casey asked.

"Well, there's this neat little town, and we can walk along the rocky coast. Very cool coastline, I'm told. We'll find stuff to do."

Casey crushed up the wrappers from McDonald's and tossed them in the nearby garbage can.

"You always say that, Dad. *We'll find stuff,*" Casey said.

"And we do, don't we?"

"Yeah, I guess so," he said with little conviction.

"Oh come on. You have to be open to something new. Something unexpected."

Without the slightest pause in the conversation, Graham responded as if I had fed him the line, told him the perfect thing to say.

"Like seeing Ali." Graham said, resting his back against his chair and pulling his GAME BOY from his pocket.

Ali was long gone. I looked down the long terminal hallway, not in a last second attempt to catch a final glimpse, but instead to remember Ali's wink.

"Okay. I get that," Casey said. "Not everybody gets to see Ali, I guess."

I gulped down the last of my coffee, reached inside my carry-on bag, and pulled out a computer printout from the website of one of Oregon's dune buggy rental shops, scanned for the phone number, and dialed my cell to make a reservation for three.

The Oregon trip was a warm-up, a practice run for the road trip we were now on. But it took a lot to get there, generations of trips, not only the ones on pavement but those of the mind, the psyche, and the soul. They have been part of an ongoing life map, an expedition into who I am, who my boys are. What's found along these roads is what illuminates the heart's dark chambers. When I spotted Ali, a light went on, and I could once again see my father.

When Dad was a teenager, he and his buddies used to beat the crap out of each other every weekend inside a makeshift boxing ring in the basement of his boyhood home. Using his mother's ball of clothesline, Dad roped off a square section of the cracked and uneven concrete floor. He put old wooden folding chairs in two of the four corners, drew a big X in the middle of the square with white chalk, and laced-up a pair of black leather boxing gloves. Three neighborhood buddies would take turns pummeling each other until their bare-chested bodies glistened with sweat. There was rarely blood, but plenty of bruises, and Dad and his friends wore the contusions like badges.

Dad never had a formal lesson. Instead, he learned the basics from listening to boxing on the radio. The *Cavalcade of Sports* broadcast Friday night matches on the NBC Radio Network in the late 1940s. St. Nicholas Arena in New York City was the venue for the earliest bouts. To a fourteen-year-old boy from a working class family outside a Pennsylvania steel town, New York might as well have been New Delhi, Amsterdam, or the Emerald City. And the announcers calling the punches were Dad's remote boxing teachers, describing each mighty wallop, each cutting blow with vivid words in hyper-pitched detail, drawing diagrams in my father's head. In his mind's eye, Dad could see the quick in-and-out action of a left jab, the perfect angle of a devastating right cross, the gloves-against-the-chin technique of defending yourself from an opponent's ferocious flurry to the head. Dad sat alone on

David W. Berner

the floor just a few feet from the cloth-covered speaker of the family's big Philco console radio, developing black-and-white mind photographs of dangerous punches and dancing feet. His eyes stayed closed, his hands punched at the air, and he swayed and jerked his head as if in a tango with the announcer's words. When the weekends came, Dad would reenact what he imagined, delivering strikes to the bodies of the boys who stepped inside his homemade ring. Dad was not a big kid. He stood only about five-and-a-half feet tall. But he had a stocky, muscular body, and broad shoulders with biceps and forearms hardened by the routine of daily pushups. It was what was between the ears that seemed to separate him from the others. Dad was not a strategic, competitive fighting genius. But he had demons rattling in his head, stirring in his gut that had nowhere else to go but straight out through his gloved fists.

Dad's father never asked for a divorce. His mother never would have agreed to it anyway. So when his father left to live with the woman in the house a block away, he was still married to my grandmother, and he was still, at least biologically, Dad's father. And before his father moved out, during the early rounds of basement boxing, Dad must have sensed the widening distance between his father and mother. He must have suffered the inner numbness that comes from sitting at silent dinner tables, trying to block out the arguments that rumbled through the house as he lay on his bed at night with his eyes closed and his hands over his ears. And in a house where stoicism was revered, crying not permitted, and daily discipline was based on the basic rule of do-what-I-say, Dad must have had nowhere else to release his emotions than inside a boxing ring. He let all

104

the anger, resentment, fear, and sorrow gather in his gut and then let it burst out in the controlled violence of a basement brawl.

Dad stopped boxing after a few years, but he never lost his love of a good fight.

When I was a boy, he would turn on nearly all the televised boxing matches. "Want to watch this with me?" he would ask. I'd sit and stare at the TV, believing it was easier to agree to sit there with him than to argue about why I didn't care about boxing.

"Can I go now?" I'd say, after just a few minutes.

"Where you going? Don't you want to see this?"

I was usually out of the room before he could ask those questions again.

Dad believed that nothing in the world could be better than locking our eyes on the grainy black-and-white images of two men pounding the snot out of each other. He couldn't imagine that his young son could find anything more interesting, more compelling to do with his time. But he never demanded I stay, and never ordered me to spend time with boxing.

This all began in the era of Cassius Marcellus Clay, the man who would later become Muhammad Ali. Clay had won the gold medal at the 1960 Olympics in Rome, and he was impossible to ignore. He was handsome and glib, relentlessly taunting his opponents with insults loaded with raging braggadocio. But to my father, Clay was arrogant, annoying, and unlikable.

"He's a smart-ass. He should shut his damn mouth." Dad said things like this directly to the television screen, waving his finger or fist. It happened every time Clay was interviewed in the days or moments before a fight. "Someone needs to rip out that guy's tongue," Dad said.

The contempt for Clay was venomous. Plenty of Whites called him a nigger, a monkey, a black boy who didn't know his place. I never heard Dad say anything like that; it never got that ugly. Dad simply couldn't stomach Clay's antics and just wanted Sonny Liston to beat the living daylights out of him. Liston was the heavyweight champion in 1964, an ex-con with a fierce, nasty reputation. Clay was the upstart twenty-two-year-old who loved the spotlight. "Liston's too ugly to be the champ," Clay said to smiling reporters during an impromptu news conference just days before the fight. The reporters loved Clay's fast-talking rants. Dad did not.

"Show it in the ring, Clay. Show it in the ring."

And almost immediately, Clay did just that, winning fights with conviction. A couple of years later, when he embraced Islam and changed his name, he seemed to only get better. And when Muhammad Ali declared himself a conscientious objector and avoided the military during the Vietnam War, Dad despised him even more.

"So, now he's a draft dodger? Jesus Christ."

Curiously though, after showing such fervent dislike of Ali, such passion for pointing out everything he believed was wrong with the man, Dad didn't stay angry. Over time, Dad seemed to realize nothing he said was going to change the man he had called "the egomaniac from Louisville, Kentucky." I'm not sure I completely understood why Dad softened his stance, especially as Ali became more outspoken on racism and the war and inevitably one of the era's lightning rods. There were fewer shouts and verbal outbursts directed at Ali's television image. For whatever reason, Dad's perception of Ali changed. It came in tiny intervals, but still, it came.

"There's no doubt the man can box," my father said, pausing for a moment. "But I'd like him more if he would just shut up now and then." Dad said this after Ali's second win over Liston and then the victory over Floyd Patterson in the mid 1960s. He said as much again after Ali returned to boxing in 1971 and lost his first professional fight to Joe Frazier. And again after Ken Norton broke Ali's jaw in 1973, and after Ali challenged Joe Frazier in 1974 and beat him to regain his heavyweight title.

By this time, Dad had stopped calling him Clay and started calling him Ali. He learned not to take Ali's trash-talking comments so seriously, and began seeing them as playful, theatrical performances with a wink. Dad thought it was the right decision to strip Ali of his heavyweight title because of his stance on the Vietnam War, but he later showed an unexpected tolerance for Ali's outspokenness even when my father didn't agree with him. Dad also started to see the distinction between Ali's religious convictions and his showmanship. My father didn't understand Islam and certainly didn't appreciate braggarts, but he was apparently beginning to recognize how Ali could blend the two into a flawless dance. Ali's incredible awareness of self, in some small way, must have started to resonate with my father. Maybe Dad's own faith, albeit tenuous and fractured, might have given him just enough conviction to rise above the pain of his own father's exit from his life. Or just maybe Dad began to realize he possessed a little of the Ali

David W. Berner

cockiness, just enough of Ali's unbridled confidence to fuel the one final punch that once silenced his opponents in that cold, damp basement boxing ring.

Six years after my father's death, Graham and I sat at the kitchen table on a Saturday morning, eating egg-white omelets and turkey sausage.

"Dad, I want to do some of that MMA fighting. Mixed martial arts," Graham said. He's been watching the fights, the Ultimate Fighting Championships, on cable television.

"You're crazy." I had seen only some of the matches, watching a little over his shoulder. I wasn't a fan. It appeared undisciplined and exceedingly violent.

"What's wrong with it?" Graham asked.

"You'll get yourself killed."

"Dad, I'm not saying I should go stick my head in the ring *now*. I need to train." Graham had been contemplating this for some time.

I stood up to pour myself another cup of coffee.

"I don't play football anymore. Maybe this kind of training would help me get into shape," Graham continued.

"I would worry each time you stepped in the ring," I said from behind the kitchen counter. "You want more milk?"

"Dad, seriously. I think I want to try this. At least train a bit, maybe with someone who knows this kind of stuff."

I took a slow sip of coffee, considering what I was about to say.

"It would be a big commitment, you know?" I said, trying to gauge how much he meant what he said.

"Hey, come on. I could carry on the family DNA," Graham said, laughing.

"Family DNA?"

"Pappy was a boxer, right?"

"Well, he didn't exactly train, he just jumped right into boxing. It wasn't supervised. I'm not going to let you just start beating on people."

"Exactly," Graham said. "That's why I should train with someone."

I didn't want to say it out loud, not in front of him, but the more Graham talked, the more I thought: *Wouldn't it be something if Graham resurrected a little of my father's passion?* Certainly, the dangers of concussions, damage to the eyes, and busted jaws were on my mind. The harsh reality of the sport had destroyed Ali's health; people died in boxing rings. Still, I could see my father smiling.

"Pappy showed me how to box, you know?"

"He did?"

When Graham was a toddler, Dad had secretly shown him the boxer's stance, where to put his gloved fists, how to throw and take a punch.

"When did he do this?" I asked.

Dad used to box with Graham in the backyard or in the basement when he and my mother were babysitting. And when he'd visit us, Dad would take Graham out on the outside deck.

"It was our little thing. Just me and Pappy."

Part of me wanted to be angry. Part of me wanted to laugh. How did I not know this was going on? How did I not know Dad was sneaking in some clandestine boxing lessons with my son? Dad must have thought I would somehow disapprove.

"Okay, I think I get that. I like that it was your *little thing*," I said, picturing my father crouched low enough to match Graham's toddler height, holding his palms up for Graham to pound his clenched fists into, and coaching Graham to keep his feet moving. And at the same time, I could see my father as a young man, shadow-boxing inside the clothesline ropes of his basement ring, punching violently into the air, ducking an imaginary opponent's right hook, jabbing his left fist against the make-believe, bare-chested body of his adversary, preparing himself for the next foe who would enter the ring.

"So, MMA. Can we look for a trainer?" Graham said.

In just a few weeks, Graham was working out at a local gym run by a former college boxing champion. I installed a seventy-five-pound heavy bag and a hanging speed bag in his mother's basement. I purchased new padded boxing gloves and protective wrist wraps. Graham watched UFC matches on TV while he worked out on the elliptical or lifted weights. He wanted inside the ropes, but it would be months before he would be ready for his first sparring match. It was tough work, and Graham would get discouraged and impatient. But somehow he always was able to reach deep inside for whatever it took to put him back on his training schedule and the boxing gloves back on his hands.

"I wish Pappy could see this," Graham said, driving hard blows into the thick training mitts I wore on my hands. Graham would pound away, sweat and groan, and I would urge him on.

He reveled in nearly knocking my arms out of their sockets, loved scaring me with his hard rights that inadvertently whizzed inches from my head. He got a kick out of seeing me wince in pain or swiftly back away to avoid a wayward swing.

One night after a workout, Graham tried to convince me to watch the TV rerun of a big fight.

"Dad, you have to see this. It's the best fight I've seen on UFC," he said, while searching for the TV clicker in the basement family room.

I didn't want to see sweat spraying from the bodies of angry men or blood oozing from the facial cuts that only gloved fists could produce. I didn't want to witness the pure, primordial aggression that forced me to cringe with every single blow. As much as Graham loved the sport, I still found it terribly unsettling to watch.

"Come on. Just sit with me for a few minutes," Graham pleaded. "You have to watch the guy in the black trunks. He is an absolute beast."

The fight began and Graham stood up from his seat. "Watch his right hand. It's so amazing." Graham became increasingly more energized, more animated as punches accumulated. "He's so quick. It's a freakin' blur."

My body stiffened, filling with tension, like it does in that split second before you trip and fall.

One of the fighters had the other pinned down on the ring's floor, sitting on him, his right fist rhythmically throwing crushing blows to the head.

"Are they allowed to do that?" I asked, turning my head away from the TV screen. This of course was not the boxing match of my father's era. This was not Ali, Frazier, or Liston. This was a new kind of fight, a new kind of sport.

"There are rules, Dad. But it's *mixed* martial arts. It's not *only* boxing," Graham said, his eyes still on the television. "Oh, he's destroying him. Did you see that move?" he added, looking back at me before his eyes quickly returned to the screen.

I'm uncertain whether Dad would have seen the true sport or the athleticism in this kind of fighting. It may have taken time for him to realize its merits, if he believed it had any at all. But there's no question Dad was in the air that night. I could sense my father reaching out, calling me to stay put, to drop anchor in front of that television set and sit right next to Graham as he let the sport he loved wrap itself around every one of his senses. Dad's dad, my grandfather, never walked down the kitchen stairs of my father's boyhood home to the concrete basement floor to witness his son throw a punch in the middle of that roped-off ring. And when my Dad started to improve, gain competence, confidence, and power, and began to deliver a commanding right and a swift left, my grandfather had already moved out of the house and down the street to another woman's home. My father's experience was now rippling through the generations, demanding I box with the ghosts of an unsettled past.

The UFC match lasted only a few minutes, but there were others after it. And so, for nearly an hour, I stayed seated on the couch right next to my son, watching every headlock, every vicious kick, every brutal punch.

Chapter 10
Burying Dogs

"Go ahead. Wet your finger, wipe the ground, and lick it." The Bonneville Salt Flats were a vast, dirty-white blanket of earth, fading off into the horizon and touching the sky. The boys were struck by the utter loneliness of the landscape, but not convinced it was really salt below their sandals.

"Okay, that's salt," said Graham, scrunching his face then wiping his hand on his shorts.

"Like sea salt," said Casey.

"Probably more like road salt," I said, turning my back to a steady breeze kicking up from the west.

The road sign directed drivers to pull off the highway only at designated areas, but we ignored it, parking the RV alone on the white ground just a short walk from The Tree of Utah, an eighty-seven-foot-high abstract sculpture created by a Swedish artist. The green and yellow balls on the tree splashed color over the stark, barren landscape. But what we found just a dozen yards from the 225-ton work of art was what kept us on the Flats for more than an hour.

Buried in the salt were dozens of beer and wine bottles, each turned upside down with the heavy ends facing the sky. Some had been gathered together, shaped into patterns, symbols of one kind or another. And scratched into the salt beside every one was a message for travelers: *Lynn and Mark Forever. Give Me Strength. Be Who You Are. Jesus Will Save Me.* It was graffiti to some, but that's not how I saw it. The markers were tributes to time spent out on the salt desert, headstones of the memories left behind by friends, lovers, or single souls who came here to reflect or celebrate with the help of drink or other mind-altering substances. The messages were purposeful, as if they were compelled to leave proof of their existence. There was nothing else that could have lured them here. We were surrounded by only dry, saline earth one hundred miles from Salt Lake and thirty miles from the tiny town of Wendover, out in the middle of bleak, empty space. Places like this must have been part of what Kerouac was talking about when he wrote of "all that raw land" in the final lines of *On the Road*. Not only the rawness of the American landscape, but maybe the raw emotion of the individual spirits who had traveled here.

"They sort of look like grave markers," said Brad, looking over his shoulder from a distance as he walked back to the RV. "Some of them have been here a long time."

"You don't think anybody's buried out here, do you Dad?" Graham asked.

"Oh, come on, Graham." Casey was quick to respond to what he believed was his brother's ridiculous question.

Graham had a tough time when my father died. Casey did, too. But Graham openly struggled at the funeral, weeping his way through it. Death was overwhelmingly final to him. I'm certain he was still questioning, like Kerouac, whether there was a place for souls to go after they leave this life. "What difference does it make after all?" Kerouac wrote in *On the Road*. He wondered about heaven and if it was simply all in the mind.

Years later Graham was with me on the morning my girlfriend's dog was scheduled to die. Cancer had eaten away at the dog's right rear leg, and for nearly two weeks the flat-coated retriever had been limping and wincing in pain, the medication no longer muting what must have been an intense and continuous throbbing. The veterinarian said it was a fast-moving disease and there was little else one could do besides amputate. Still, that was no guarantee. The cancer would likely return somewhere else in the dog's body. The appointment for the injection was set for 9:40 in the morning.

Trude had two dogs. Phoenix was the older, a big lumbering animal with dark sad eyes and a love of water. When he was at his best, during his daily walks, he would race through the manicured grass on the local golf course and dive into the pond on the sixteenth fairway. He'd swim in circles, dunk his head a few times, and come out of the water only after being coaxed, shaking the droplets from the oil on his coat. This is how I would best remember Phoenix. When Trude telephoned that morning to ask if I would mind waiting to come up to her home until after the appointment at the vet to give her, her son, and daughter some time to grieve alone, I pictured Phoenix standing on the edge of the pond, among the cattails, soaking wet, quivering with indecision, trying to choose between obeying the call of his master or the pure instinctive pleasure of one more swim.

Trude's phone call came just as I was returning home from walking one of my own dogs, also one of two. Mike was a six-year-old female Labrador whose masculine name came from the nickname of a nurse who had cared for my father when Dad was receiving chemotherapy treatments. Michelle said people had called her Mike for as long as she could remember. She was a sweet lady. Mike was a sweet dog.

I filled Mike's water bowl, patted her on the top of the head, and turned toward Graham who had slept through the night on the living room couch.

"Graham!" I said, raising my voice enough to awaken, but not to alarm.

Graham was staying at my home while his mother was out-of-town. He had fallen asleep on the sofa late the previous evening while watching *Rambo* on DVD, and his body was now taking up most of the cushion space with his broad shoulders and thick, muscular thighs, his skin seemingly melting into the leather like butter on warm toast.

"Whaaa," he mumbled, his voice saturated with sleep and muffled by the three sofa pillows stuffed around his head.

"We're going to the DMV. Let's rock-n-roll." I had promised, if we had time that morning, I'd take him to get his driving permit.

"Cool," he said, rubbing his eyes and shifting from lying on his stomach to his back.

"But you've got to get up now," I said, standing over him. I could be a bit of a drill sergeant when it was time to start the day. Graham, on the other hand, tended to crawl his way into the morning. "I'm up. I'm up," he said, peeling his body from the couch, running one hand through his shoulder-length hair and the other against his belly.

"Let's get going," I said. "I want to head up north to be around for support after they put Phoenix down."

"Phoenix is dying today?" Graham asked, startled.

"Kind of strange to put it that way, but yes," I said, trying somehow to come to terms with how planned and programmed this all seemed.

"Wow," Graham said softly, stumbling through a half-hearted attempt to find his jeans and shoes. Earlier in the week, I had told him what the dog's fate would likely be, but now that the actual day was here it had become surreal. "Wouldn't it be weird to know the day you were going to die?" Graham added.

"I don't think Phoenix knows," I answered.

"Yeah, but *we* know," Graham said, pulling a freshly washed tee-shirt over his head. "I'm going to miss Phoenix. He was my buddy."

Graham dog-sat Phoenix a few times as a favor and had spent an afternoon or two with him over the last several months. "I just think he was a great guy," Graham said. "Kind of goofy, like a big oaf, but I loved him. I'm going to miss him."

"You really liked that dog, huh?" I asked, sympathetically, but surprised by Graham's reaction.

"He was the coolest. It's just sad," Graham said. "Where're they going to bury him?"

"Cremation," I said.

David W. Berner

"Burn him? Really?"

"Yes, they want to spread the ashes, maybe in his favorite park."

Graham sat up on the couch, his active eyes quietly softening into a stare. Not one of blank thought, but one of singular focus.

"When *you* die, Dad, no one better burn you." Graham said.

"Why not, Graham?"

"I just don't like thinking about it. All that heat, the burning, the flames."

"I haven't really thought about this much, Graham." I grabbed my jacket and car keys from the coffee table.

"Seriously, Dad," Graham said, still sitting on the couch, his head now raised up, his neck stiffening, his shoulders back. "Don't do it, okay?" He locked his eyes on mine. "Just don't."

I took a seat beside him on the couch and stroked my hand across Mike's back, who had wiggled her body and her continuously wagging tail between the coffee table and the right arm of the sofa. Graham grabbed the dog just below her two ears, one hand on either side, and vigorously massaged her skin and fur.

"Hey, Mike," Graham said, lowering his head so he could have a straight-on look into the dog's deep, espresso-brown eyes and shifting his vocal tone from the serious to silly, the way one does when talking to an infant. "Who's my girl? Who is my girrrllll?"

I leaned on the back cushion of the couch and thought about how several years ago Graham wept at my father's funeral, struggled with the death of my cousin's drug overdose, and wondered aloud about his grandmother's failing health, her frequent doctor appointments and hospital stays. Graham wore his emotions like badges, shining on his chest, his sorrows, worries, and joys served up like offerings to those willing to accept them without condition. And like an arm wrapping around the shoulders of a troubled friend, Mike put her nose on Graham's knee and let out a soft sigh.

Graham, like me, was a dog person. Part of that condition is hardwired, innate, and another part is pure experience. If you grow up with a dog, live with a dog, then almost through osmosis the dog becomes a vital ingredient of your existence. I had a dog in my life from the time I was a baby. The first was a Collie, given to me by my grandfather when I was just a few months old. Sally never left my side. She nestled her nose under my infant chin while on my blanket on the living room floor, circled and guarded me when I played baseball in the backyard, and slept silently and calmly when I rested my head on her belly each Saturday morning while I watched TV cartoons. And after thirteen years of companionship, on a humid and sunny Fourth of July, after several days of labored breathing and a complete loss of appetite, Sally died of old age. My father cried as he dug the grave.

"Damn fireworks," he muttered as he stabbed his spade into the soft ground under the towering white pine of our front yard.

Sally hated the cracks and pops of firecrackers, cherry bombs, and M-80s. The explosive sounds pierced her ears, sent her scurrying from the noise, cowering in a dark corner of our basement, hoping somehow to quiet the constant bangs and bursts.

She was the first dog my parents buried in our yard. In the suburb of Pittsburgh where I grew up, it was illegal to bury anything on your property, but that didn't stop my family from putting Sally, Soupy, Saddie, Gypsy, Molly, and Bob in the ground on our quarter-acre lot. My father buried the dogs under a couple of old maples, another under a big rhododendron, one by the south fence lined with forsythia, and another next to Sally under the front yard pine. Each time a dog died my father dug a hole, lined it with lime, placed or dragged the pet's body down into it, spread more lime, and completed the job with shovels of dirt.

"She hated that damn noise," my father said under his breath as he shoveled earth, soft clay, and small rocks with a quicker pace, his face flushing, the volume of his voice increasing with each toss. "She hates this. Jesus Christ, stop shooting off the goddamn firecrackers!" he shouted to the sky.

I watched from the steps of the front porch as my father finished his job, stunned, even frightened by what had unfolded just a few feet before me. There were tears I hadn't seen before, angry words aimed toward God, and an anxiety I hadn't felt before. My father's steadfast calm had disappeared. Raw emotion, vulnerability, his own insecurities, all that he had stoically tried to mask in an attempt to secure his young son's emotional safety had evaporated. The forty-year-old memory of the day my father dug Sally's grave continues to surface at unexpected times, arises from the mind's attic in unexplained flashes, in photographic form, pictures from a camera. And when it does, I not only see my beloved dog, the Collie I grew up with, the pet that would rarely leave a little boy's side, but I also see my father, the beads of sweat on his brow, tamping the last shovels of earth on a mound under a soaring evergreen tree. It's the kind of memory—the dead pet and a grieving family—that so often surfaces in the storyline of sentimentalized fiction, exploitable emotions used to pull the easily accessible string dangling from the heart. But, the experience is forever authentic, deeply human, and far more meaningful than what might be evoked in the pages of a sappy novel or a corny Hollywood tearjerker. The death of my dog, like the death of my father's stoicism, is woven into my life in complex herringbone patterns, the back-and-forth weave of a sturdy, reliable garment worn over and over.

I stood from the couch and slapped Graham on the back. "All right, let's do it. Let's get you legal."

"Let's drive!" Graham growled with enthusiasm, the way an athlete gets psyched-up with his teammates before a game.

I gave Mike a little scratch behind the right ear as I moved from the couch toward the door. "You know, Graham. If you don't cremate me, you'll have to bury me. And maybe I should be buried in the backyard at your grandmother's with all the dogs."

"I don't think there's room," Graham said, laughing.

"Maybe you could bury me on top of one of them, or build a tomb, a mausoleum. Dig up the dogs, put us all in there."

"Okay, you're getting goofy now, Dad."

"Come on. Who else would you want to spend eternity with than your most trusted friends ever?"

Graham knew I was being silly, trying to lighten the mood of the morning. He looked at me, tilted his head, put a smirk on his face and his hands on his hips. "Dad. You are too freakin' weird."

"Seriously, you could put the names of each of us on the tomb. *Here lie Sally, Soupy, Saddie, Gypsy, Molly, Bob…and DAD.*"

We laughed, forgetting for a moment what the day would eventually bring, the reality of a difficult goodbye. And Mike, sensing only the pleasure in the room the uncanny way dogs often do, quickly stood from her lying position and twisted her way in between us, her tail wagging her entire body, her ears folding slightly toward her back, and her mouth open, allowing her thick, pink tongue to fall out from the side of her snout as if she too were laughing.

The first time we rolled the windows down, we were somewhere on the California side of Lake Tahoe, sufficiently road weary, drained from the withering 100-degree heat in Utah. We knew we wouldn't make San Francisco until after dark even though we had hoped to arrive at the RV park near the bay as the sun went down. Climbing a California mountain road, I said, "Turn the AC off. It's time to let the clean air flow!" Brad and I cranked the windows down and the boys moved in close behind our cab seats to catch the wind.

We could see the sinking sun through our windshield as we hit walls of traffic just outside San Francisco. As Brad drove, I thumbed through our trip's copy of *On the Road* and found the passage where Sal Paradise talks about the white city of San

Francisco and its "potato-patch fog." Kerouac had come into the bay area through Oakland, different than our trip. But I was feeling the same beauty before me. Only our arrival was without the city's famous fog. Instead, we were wrapped inside a clear night sprinkled with sparkling city lights.

Our road map to the RV lot near the old football stadium was crude and outdated, and after several misguided turns and verbal clashes over directions, we finally found the dimly lit entrance to our trailer park home.

"Ah huh," the security guard grunted from inside the shed on the park's short driveway next to San Francisco Bay. That was about as much greeting he was going to give anyone who rudely awakened him from his nightly nap.

"Number 9," he groaned, and then paused for what seemed like minutes.

"And number 9 is where?" I asked, breaking the silence, assuming that number likely represented our parking space.

"Number 9. Yep, number 9. You've got number 9."

No matter what we asked, his response was the same. "Number 9. Yep, 9." Reciting these numbers was clearly a habit, like a tick, a way to remember the space we rented. He repeated it more than a dozen times.

When we pulled away from the entrance, Casey and Graham burst into laughter.

"That guy is hilarious," said Casey, choking out his words.

"*Number 9, number 9*," said Graham, mimicking the guard. "Is that all he can say? *Number 9, number 9*. What a nutcase."

Graham had always been quick to laugh, a jokester, a kid who could repeat every line from a *Saturday Night Live* skit.

David W. Berner

Graham couldn't remember school homework assignments, but he could recite every line of dialogue from a Chris Farley routine. Casey was different, more reluctant to show his softer side. He was a happy kid. But unlike Graham, laughter was not as easily ignited. Casey was disciplined about his emotions, his schoolwork, and his passions. It fueled his personality.

The boys joked about the exchange at the gate for more than an hour, all of us repeating the story with added absurdity with each telling. We had been on the road for just short of a week, enjoying the subdued contentment of days of highway driving and dazzling scenery, some chuckles and smiles, but this was our first eye-watering, belly-rumbling laugh. Brad and I forgot all about Kerouac, Graham forgot all about the RV not being a sports car, and Casey forgot all about his cameras.

We had come a long way from the Salt Flats and those beer bottle memorials, more than a thousand miles from Denver and all the *On the Road* connections, and more than two thousand from my home in Chicago. But in many ways, it was our arrival in San Francisco that was the true inauguration of our journey. Any of the anxiety I once harbored about the boys buying into the idea of this road trip faded that night thanks to a San Francisco security guard with a quirky routine for remembering numbers.

Chapter 11
Giving God the Finger

Everyone had made a mental directory of things to see on the first full day in San Francisco: Golden Gate Park, cable cars, Lombard Street, The Haight, Chinatown, Alcatraz. But I was the only one with City Lights Bookstore on his list. I was able to persuade the others to head out for the North Beach neighborhood first thing in the morning.

City Lights was a Bohemian shrine, and on the drive there I took it upon myself—with obvious risk—to give Brad and the boys a little background about the place. After all, it was the western home of the Beats, and the Kerouac links were numerous.

"When you go inside you'll think about growing a goatee," I said, using an old beatnik cliché.

"Like yours, Dad?" Graham asked.

"Well, the true beatnik goatee was just that little ball of fur on the chin," I said. "No mustache part."

"I think we should all just grow them for the trip," said Brad. "Come on, let's do it. Casey, you in?"

"Ah, no," Casey said. "I'll stay whisker-less, thanks." Ironically, years later he would grow a full beard.

"I'll do it," said Graham.

"Hate to tell you, Grambo," Brad said, "I don't think we'll be in California long enough to get something going on that baby-ass chin of yours."

"At least I'm not bald," Graham snapped. Clearly it was a jab at me. My sons had a million bald jokes.

From my early college days, I gravitated to the haphazardness of establishments like City Lights—book stores, record shops—places that had the energy, the essence of a living thing, and the odd mix of chaos and convention. Most of the books at City Lights were arranged on floor-to-ceiling shelves. Others were stacked on the floor and tucked into tight crannies, places one could hide for hours devouring prose and poetry. The old pockmarked wooden floors creaked and the walls were littered with handwritten signs and posters of left-leaning political causes. City Lights seemed a careless and caring place at the same time, and it carried a reverence, like a literary church. Inside, I walked slowly and spoke softly, just as one would in the halls of a temple.

It wasn't quite the same experience for the boys.

Brad had found interest in the endless photos—Kerouac, Ginsberg, Dylan—and had gravitated upstairs to the poetry section. Graham saw City Lights as just another tourist stop, holding marginal interest. However, the look of the place did appeal to him—the handwritten signs on the walls like *Books not Bombs* and the City Lights tee-shirts, black with simple white lettering. "Pretty neat, Dad," he said. Although I tried to excite Graham with the history and significance of City Lights, people watching was far more interesting. How could a boy not get a kick out of the old hippies, the North Beach punks, the tattooed and pierced, the homeless walking along Columbus Avenue and Jack Kerouac Alley?

As for Casey, he was willing to accept my exuberance over City Lights, but didn't share it. However, it did seem he had some tepid interest as long as he could see the visual story in it. So I tried to help. *See this over here*, I said, looking into his lens and pointing to a sign promoting a poetry reading. It had been Scotch-taped to City Light's front door. *Look at this*, I said, coaxing him and his camera toward the bookstore's large picture window.

"Dad, you're always a little *on*," he said while holding the cup of the viewfinder to his eye. "But you're getting better. You have to try to talk, like, you know…*normal*."

I thought I was pretty natural on camera. He thought differently and needed to tell me so.

Casey ate up a lot of digital video space outside City Lights, focusing on the door and the people coming and going with books under their arms, on Kerouac's prose stamped on the large City Lights window, on the Kerouac Alley sign, and on his father standing silently on the sidewalk, admiring what was before him.

"Did you get everything?" I asked, looking back at the camera.

He was silent.

"Casey?" I said directly into the lens.

Still silent.

"Case?" I asked again as he moved in tighter, the camera now uncomfortably close.

Casey's finger pushed the stop button. He held the camera with one hand and removed it from his right eye.

"Got it," Casey said. "You're better, you know, when you don't know I'm filming you." He moved the camera back to his eye to capture more people walking the streets. "We've been all around this place now, so how about I go inside with the camera now?"

That was a problem.

City Lights management wouldn't let Casey enter with any photographic equipment, but he was never one to embrace authority if he saw holes in the argument. Like Sal Paradise and Dean Moriarty, Casey was ready to question, challenge, even reject the rules, if the only argument was *because someone said so.*

What possible harm could a camera do?

I'd be discreet, unobtrusive.

What's the worst they could do, throw me out?

Casey snuck the camera through the door, filming surreptitiously from his hip. A part of me believes City Lights would have praised him for ignoring policy.

I had always encouraged the boys, beginning with the time they felt wronged by a grade on an elementary school test, to question authority. And although it took me until adulthood to see the connection, I knew challenging the powerful and the status quo came directly from my mother—one of the first in our neighborhood to openly speak out at picnics and card club meetings about how Vietnam was wrong. Some of it came from my father. Dad was more conservative in his politics than Mom, but when it was time to speak out, especially when someone's misguided rule or decision was impacting his family, he was right there on the firing line.

When I was a boy, just after my Holy Communion, I stood just outside the front door of our church, wondering why Dad's face was so red.

"Just wait here, David. Do not move from this spot," my father said sternly, pointing to my feet and the ground where I stood.

Earlier that morning, Dad and I had taken our usual place in the back near the windows of St. Alexander Church, while my mother and sister found seats in the crowded pews near the altar. In that way, the day was like all the other Sundays before it, except on this morning each of us had planned to say a few extra prayers.

It had been only a few days since our family buried my grandmother. Nanny was my mother's mother—a lively, devilish woman who dropped five teaspoons of sugar in my tea when my mother wasn't looking, insisted the secret ingredient in her homemade potato soup was a mouthful of her spit, and routinely shoved the knuckle of her right index finger tight against her nostril, pretending to pick boogers from her nose. "E-ooh!" my sister and I would yell. Nanny would laugh and tickle us at the armpits. "I don't pick my nose, you goofballs," she would giggle, showing us her clean fingertip. "But I bet *you* do!" she would shout, continuing to tickle us until we squirmed in frantic attempts to escape.

Nanny had a Lucky Strike every morning with her coffee, the blue smoke of the tobacco and white smoke of her Maxwell

David W. Berner

House mixing together just inches from her thin face. She'd have many more Luckies during the day, matching each one with another cup of black coffee. She loved smoking, the ritual of tapping the cigarette's filter on the table before lighting it, the sharp smell of sulfur from the matches, and that first stinging but satisfying inhale. When she died, my mother put a full carton of Lucky Strikes in the coffin, praying the angels would let her smoke in Heaven. Knowing Nanny, she had all intentions of puffing away in the presence of God.

I could see my father move, almost march his way from the church entrance and down the concrete walkway, maneuvering deliberately around the parishioners in their dark sport coats, spring dresses, and Sunday hats. He squeezed by an elderly woman with a cane, never saying *excuse me,* never once looking back my way.

At the end of the walkway near the parking lot, stood Father John. He was in his white linen surplice and the clerical collar that peeked up at the neck. He shook hands and talked with churchgoers, smiling and touching children on the head. Father John was a tall, white-haired priest with straight-back posture and a reputation for running his church with the sternness of an old-school baseball manager—enthusiasm for the game, but insistent about the results. He often quoted from the Bible in casual conversations, regularly at mass, or anytime he believed his parishioners needed it. Father John once visited my Sunday school class moments before an exam on Moses and the Ten Commandments. He could have recited any number of Bible verses that morning, but even though I don't remember exactly what he said, I'd bet it was the one he often delivered to the public school kids who attended catechism.

"He who ignores discipline despises himself, but whoever heeds correction gains understanding."

Father John stood inches from the front row of classroom desks, his eyes closed, his deep, resonate voice echoing off the walls.

"That proverb, my children, each of you should remember today."

He stared at us children, and then turned and walked from the room, leaving behind a silent vacuum.

Father John also talked a great deal about money. Not to the Sunday school students, but to the parishioners. This was what really rattled Dad. There was a time when my father complained about it regularly, telling my mother, "Is that all he can ever talk about? Give me cash," Dad said. "Jesus Christ. I'm not printing money in the basement!" If you asked Dad, money was the subject of every single one of Father John's Sunday sermons. "Is this what church has come to? How much money you give?" Dad would say.

I was too far away to hear my Father's exact words, but I could see him step up to Father John and begin to speak, his hands on his hips, his face still flushed. Dad leaned in closer and raised an accusatory index finger, nearly touching the priest's left shoulder. Father John stood almost a foot taller than Dad, but he still backed away from my father apparently stunned by Dad's sudden forcefulness. The air between them seemed to spark like the sputtering wick of a dangerously faulty

David W. Berner

firecracker. Parishioners turned their heads toward Dad and the priest, and several moved quickly aside, creating an immediate distance.

I ducked behind the glass doors of the church, as if trying to protect myself from an explosion, and peered through the crack where the door met the jamb. Father John grabbed my father's arm, directing him down the walkway closer to the church entrance and away from the remaining parishioners. As the two of them moved, I began to hear my father's words.

"And I don't understand who the hell you think you are?" said Dad, both of them now standing halfway between the church doors and the end of the sidewalk.

"Norman, please," said Father John.

There's that moment before an angry man throws a punch, when his facial muscles appear to constrict and blood rushes to his eyes. I knew the look. I saw it at the school playground when my friend Joey took a big swing at Matthew, accusing him of kissing the girl with the blonde curls. Unlike Joey, I didn't believe Dad would throw a punch, but he certainly had the look of someone poised for a fight.

"I'm not settling down," Dad said, yanking his arms from the priest's grip. "You call yourself a man of God. But you won't allow a good woman to be remembered by your church because of *money*?"

"It's not that simple, Norman. There are rules and obligations to the church. As the Bible says: Wealth quickly gotten dwindles away, but…"

"Bullshit," my father exploded.

I was now certain my father was going to Hell. When a classmate would act out against the nuns in my religion classes—talk back to them, show disrespect—they were told to fall to their knees and pray to God for forgiveness. But this was worse. Dad *swore at a priest*. It was as if Dad had given God the finger.

I leaned against the wall, keeping my eyes focused through the door's crack.

"It's policy, Norman."

"Policy? God's policy? I don't think so."

"I'm sorry you feel this way," Father John said calmly, but firmly.

"Don't expect to get another cent from me or my family. Don't expect us to show up at your church," my father said, unbuttoning his sport jacket and hiking up his slacks the way he would when his stained painter pants would slip on his waist while doing odd jobs around the house.

There came a brief, uneasy pause in the argument. Dad sighed, shook his head, and said, "Something is very wrong here. And you? Well, you should be ashamed."

Dad turned away from Father John and called my name. "David!" I was frozen, frightened to move. I slithered out from behind the door, looking down at the concrete pavement. Dad took hold of my hand. "Let's go," he said, yanking me up the walkway and marching his way out to the parking lot and into our car.

More than a year before, my grandmother had stopped attending mass because of her health and she had not given a weekly offering to the church for quite a long time. St. Alexander had apparently kept meticulous records. There was never a formal funeral mass for Nanny at St. Alexander, and my father would never again return to regular Sunday masses. Neither would my mother. And me? After years of avoiding anything that had to do with religion, I fell in love with an Irish Catholic girl and agreed to be married in a Catholic Church, a grand cathedral in Erie, Pennsylvania. It was the first church service I remembered attending in nearly twenty years. We raised our children as Catholics. Then, twelve years later, we disobeyed church doctrine, ignored the sacrament, and legally divorced under the rules of the state of Illinois.

Lately, I've been reading about Native American spirituality and Buddhism, and hoping there is a heaven.

Just a couple blocks down Columbus Avenue from City Lights was the Sentinel Building. The structure was pie-shaped and ornate with a rounded façade and copper green finish distinguishing it from the structures to its left and right. The steel frame of the building survived the 1906 earthquake. This was Francis Ford Coppola's place. It was the film director's North Beach studio and wine restaurant. On the upper floors was Zoetrope Studios where it's believed he made the final edits of *Apocalypse Now,* and on the first floor was Coppola's understated wine café.

After hours at City Lights and a group photograph outside the front door, we all needed some lunch.

The restaurant's tables were covered with white linen tablecloths and Italian opera played through the speakers. We took a table in the back near a wall rack of wine next to a two-person table by the window and a set of stairs leading to a basement. From below a waitress came.

"Did you see him?" she whispered as I squeezed around another table to get to my seat.

"See him?" I asked.

"Francis. Francis is on the patio."

"Coppola?"

"Yeah, he was upstairs working on something. He came down for lunch."

The waitress wanted us to wait while she slyly checked if the director was still enjoying his food and a glass of wine. Instead, we followed her, all four of us in a line trying not to look conspicuous. It wasn't working.

"He's been upstairs all morning, editing, I guess," the waitress said in a whisper, turning her head to us as she walked. "Some new project."

Before our Kerouac trip, I had read somewhere that Coppola had been considering producing a screenplay of *On the Road*. Could the great filmmaker be working on that project in the rooms just above our heads? Although I had absolutely no way to confirm this fantasy of mine, I couldn't ignore it. Here we were on a Kerouac journey to San Francisco, and we end up in Coppola's restaurant while he edits his way through the early filming of a screenplay of Kerouac's masterpiece. I wanted it to be true.

"Is he out there?" I asked the waitress, looking anxiously toward Casey. I knew he'd love to get a peek at the bulky and bearded film icon.

"He *was*," she said, whispering again, looking through the double doorway to the patio, her head moving back and forth to survey the outside eating area. "Let me take another look." She winked at us and headed outside to a section not easily seen from our vantage point.

"Can you imagine?" I said, turning to Brad. "How wild is this?"

I stuck my head out toward the patio, trying to see the waitress.

"You see him, Dad?" Graham asked, knowing Coppola was someone famous, but not really knowing why.

"No, nobody's out here," I said.

"We've got to look pretty geeky standing around looking for Coppola," Casey wondered aloud, concerned we were taking on the appearance of a gang of crazy fans.

"I guarantee we are not the first," said Brad, "and so what if we look *geeky*."

The waitress appeared from around the other side of the patio, snapping the middle finger and thumb of her right hand. "Damn, he's gone," she said. "But he *was* there."

"Could he be coming back? Maybe he just went to the bathroom?" I asked at the risk of sounding like an obsessed admirer. Casey rolled his eyes, a silent comment on what he thought of my overzealous interest. Still, the video camera remained in Casey's hand, trigger finger on the record button.

If there was a chance to capture Coppola, he wasn't going to miss it.

"Hold on," She turned to a server on his way past with a plate of calamari and asked, "Che successo a Francesco?" Without stopping, the server gave a quick, definitive answer. We needed no translation. We knew we had missed him.

No one said a word until we sat back down at our table. Casey turned off his camera, attached the lens cover, and set the camera down on the floor directly between my chair and his. He put his hand on my shoulder for just a moment, the kind of intimate gesture that didn't always come so easily.

"It's okay, Dad," he said, seeing I was disappointed. "It was pretty awesome just to get this close."

At that moment I wanted to believe Casey knew exactly what I was thinking. I wanted him to understand and accept my reasons for taking this trip, to know why I was determined to re-examine myself, to know why I tried to chase down Coppola, to realize that traveling in the spirit of Kerouac might have been what I wanted, but what Casey wanted mattered too, and mattered even more.

For days and nights our road adventure had pulled us west to the Pacific Ocean, more than two thousand road miles to San Francisco and an accidental respite at Zoetrope. This was exactly where we were supposed to be—the boys eating pasta, Brad and I drinking Coppola's wine, talking about our favorite scenes in *Apocalypse Now*, considering what actors might play the key roles in an *On the Road* movie, and keeping a watchful eye on the steps to the upstairs studio.

Chapter 12
Music and the
Art of Car Repair

At the corner of Haight and Ashbury, a man sat crossed-legged on the sidewalk, chanting like a monk.

"Okay, maybe just a *little* drugs," said Casey from across the street.

A few others—young, old, men, and women began to gather around the middle-aged man with the long hair and untidy beard, and hold hands.

"I don't think so," I said.

"Really? Come on," said Brad. "High as shit."

I couldn't be certain, but this crowd did not seem to me to be fueled by drugs. It was instead a ritual, a spontaneous moment in praise of the day, life, The Haight, God, Buddha, something. This was above drugs, something beyond, but I couldn't put my finger on it.

Casey snapped a photo.

Our second day in San Francisco was a tourists' day. We left the RV at the trailer park, rented a car, and headed for the Golden Gate Bridge, Lombard Street, and lunch in Sausalito where finding an open restaurant was made more difficult by a midday power outage. Although it wasn't necessarily on the must-see list for the boys, The Haight was on mine. I had been in the district once before, during my undergraduate days. I hung out with my college girlfriend along the strip of hippie stores and nearby Golden Gate Park, and stood outside the house where the members of Grateful Dead once lived. I wanted to return to share a little of the experience with my sons, and what was happening on the corner of Haight and Ashbury was far more authentic than what the rest of The Haight had become.

"So this place was like Hippie Heaven?" asked Graham.

"Yeah, I guess you could say that. Peace and love. But there was a dark side too. A lot of runaway kids and serious drug issues, way beyond a joint or two."

"Like that guy," said Casey, nodding at the cross-legged man.

Commercialization now permeated much of The Haight, capitalizing on what it once was. The *yuppie* had moved into *hippie* territory, and to many, what was happening on the corner in front of us now seemed less real, a sideshow act performed by old hippies and wanna-be Bohemians with nothing better to do. Still, pieces of that tie-dyed, incense burning, acid-dropping past remained in a few of the shops. One of them—I think it was simply called Peace—sold inexpensive posters and painted artwork with beautiful Zen writings. I bought one with a message on individualism, believing in who you are, and finding your life's work. Brad bought another with a different message, but I don't remember what it said. I also purchased some incense sticks for Graham. All of us loved Amoeba Music, a huge store with hundreds of racks of CDs and vinyls covering the floor of the former bowling alley. We spent hours inside. I left with an early Dylan record, *Another Side of Bob Dylan,* still in its original cellophane. But mostly the boys found The Haight to be little more than strangely quaint, and tolerated Dad's interest in it. That was okay. I once had been on their side of the father-son push-and-pull.

We had a one-car garage in my boyhood home with plenty of grease on the concrete floor. There was a small spot, black with a translucent purple film around the edges on the ground where petroleum had dripped from the oil pan of my father's Pontiac. On the shelf against the rear wall were two toolboxes, one of them once belonged to my grandfather and the other was Dad's. Each overflowed with tools; so many, neither of the lids could be closed. And underneath the car was my father, lying on a rectangular piece of plywood to protect him from the grimy floor, holding a Craftsman wrench in his greasy hand.

"Pass me the pliers on the ground there," Dad said from beneath the front end of the vehicle. I heard him, but all I could see were dark brown work boots, sticking out from the automobile's shadow cast on the concrete. It reminded me of that scene from *The Wizard of Oz* where the Wicked Witch of the East is smashed under Dorothy's tornado-twisted house, only the witch's feet protruding from underneath.

I gave him the pliers. "How much longer, Dad?"

There was no answer to the question. Instead there was another request. "On the shelf near the tool boxes—see those other pliers? They have silver handles. Get me those."

David W. Berner

I pushed myself up from the floor and shuffled to the shelving.

Dad could sense my sour mood. He'd seen it before. "David," he said, his voice echoing slightly from below the open hood of his 1969 Fury, "Don't you want to learn something about cars?"

"Well…not really," I said from the other side of the garage, picking up the tool he had asked me to retrieve. *It doesn't feel like I'm really learning anything anyway. I'm just handing Dad tools. What's there to learn?*

I reached under the car and handed him what he needed.

"It's okay," he said, stretching an arm out to grab the pliers, still on his back, his eyes on his work. "You don't have to be out here."

I didn't have any idea what he was trying to fix and didn't bother to ask. From the moment he drafted me to help, I ached to be far away from the garage's odorous cocktail of gasoline and grease. Instead, I wanted to be on the other side of the door to the basement, seated at the big upright grand piano.

"You sure, Dad?"

"Go," he said, still buried under the car.

The piano was deep brown trimmed in what appeared to be cherry wood. It had real ivory keys, yellowed by age. Of the three floor pedals, only two operated correctly. And the piano was perpetually out of tune, off-key enough that most anyone, even someone with only a reasonably developed ear, would have noticed. Dad bought the piano from an elderly woman who was a client of his when he worked in the insurance business.

He gave her thirty-five dollars for it, and it was up to Dad to get it out of her house. Not an easy job. But Dad had a plan.

"Meet me at my office around one o'clock on Thursday afternoon," he said to two of his buddies, refusing to enlighten them with any more than that. They were good enough friends not to ask, showing up without questions. "Gentlemen," he said when they arrived, "you're going to help me move a piano."

Dad rented a pickup truck, and for most of the afternoon the three pushed, pulled, and heaved the piano out of the lady's home, lugging it only a few feet at a time, resting their bodies, and then lugging it again. They somehow lifted it into the truck bed, probably with some sort of improvised ramp device, drove the truck several miles and up the steep driveway of our house. My father had to remove the basement's door jamb in order to squeeze the massive instrument through the door and maneuver it against the just-long-enough basement wall directly adjacent to the outside door. Dad and his friends, foreheads glistening from perspiration and shirts discolored from the stain of sweat, sat on the floor and drank bottles of Budweiser, silently staring at the hulking upright. They knew that piano would be the reason they would have aching muscles the next morning.

I sat on the piano stool and played a C-chord, then thumbed a C-note an octave below the piano's middle, letting the sound ring out. I knew Dad could hear the music, albeit muffled by a nearly closed basement door. Simultaneously, I heard the muted sounds of metal on metal, tools on steel, the notes of a countermelody coming from the other side of the door to the garage. I shaped my fingers into a simple G-chord

David W. Berner

and again thumbed a G-note one octave lower, allowing the clanging from the garage to fill in the harmonic spaces.

Months before this, when I told my parents I was interested in playing the piano, they never hesitated to set up lessons, drive me seven miles every Tuesday night to Spratt's Music, and pay ten dollars for the half-hour instruction. Mom spent hours looking in the classified sections of the local papers for a used upright. But it was Dad who found the piano of my childhood, the one on which I practiced my scales, on which I would eventually play Beethoven's "Fur Elise," on which I would later develop the skills to play Scott Joplin and George Gershwin.

I played a D-chord, rooted in the D-note just above middle C, and used the baby finger of my left hand to play the D bass note. The easy chords were about as far as I could stretch my talents at the age of twelve, five months since my inaugural lesson.

"David." I heard my father call from the garage. "Come on out here for a minute."

What did he want now? I thought I was done with this car stuff, handing him things, being his car repair slave.

"I'm coming," I said, closing my eyes and hoping he wasn't again going to ask me to help fetch tools. I stood just inside the door to the basement, arms hanging by my sides, shoulders slumping.

My father crawled out from under his car, wiped his oily hands with an already stained rag, unaware of a smudge of black grease on his left cheek about an inch below the eye. He rubbed the sweat from his forehead with his muscular right forearm.

"Can you play that one song with the da-da-da in it? Oh, how's it go again?" Dad said, frustrated he couldn't immediately recall it. "You know, da-da-da, di-di-di. It's the one you learned last week. Something from your lesson, I think?"

I knew the song. I knew where my fingers were supposed to go. And as Dad climbed back under his car, I returned to the basement, found my Mel Bay music book in the pile of sheet music on the basement floor, rested it on the piano's stand, and began to play a simple song on a big piano so difficult to haul that maneuvering it into its new home nearly crushed my father's toes and smashed his fingers; a piano once adorned with frilly doilies yellowed with age and faded photographs in heavy brass frames; a piano that for years had been silent in the living room of an elderly lady's home; an instrument that forty years later, twenty years after I had moved out of my parent's house, and six years after my father's death, would be sold again for thirty-five dollars to a another father with a U-haul truck and a young son who also had asked if he could learn to play the piano.

After riding the cable cars, we had dinner at Fisherman's Wharf and took a late night cab back to our parked car.

"Where you guys from?" the cabbie asked with a soft, childlike voice, the antithesis of his burly physique.

"Boys and I are from Chicago. He's from Denver," I replied, pointing to Brad.

"Love Denver. What brings you here?"

"We're on a little road trip. Reread *On the Road* and decided to head out."

145

"Oh, wow. I read that so many years ago. Loved it. You know, I really need to read that again."

"Good plan."

"I definitely need to do that. Yeah, *On the Road,* wow," he said. He stopped the cab at a red light and waved a teenage boy and his girlfriend through the crosswalk. "Have you been to City Lights?"

"Yesterday," I said.

"Lawrence Ferlinghetti is the richest communist there is," the cabbie said, laughing.

Ferlinghetti opened City Lights and its publishing company in 1953 and had always been an ardent lefty.

We told the cabbie about our stops in Denver and Utah, and where we were headed next—Big Sur, Arizona, Santa Fe. And he offered his story of dropping out of corporate America, becoming a cab driver, and never looking back.

"No regrets. Wouldn't change a thing," he said. "Here's your corner, fellas."

"Thanks so much," I said, stepping out into the street, "and remember to read Kerouac again."

"Hey, thanks for reminding me of that book. I have an old copy somewhere on my shelf at home, and it will be in front of my eyes later tonight."

Brad tipped the cabbie ten dollars. We drove our rented car back to the RV park, the boys asleep in the back seat.

146

Chapter 13
Exploding Boy

My sister started playing guitar before I did, but gave it up after three lessons. I gleaned a few things by secretly watching the living room lessons from the other side of the kitchen door, and then fiddling around with her cheap Kmart six-string until I could play a simple progression of chords. It was my freshman year of high school and I had just enough musical background—trombone in the school band and piano lessons—to stumble my way through. I saved $250 from my summer job as a greenskeeper's assistant at a local nine-hole golf course, bought a steel string Yamaha, and started playing rock with a few school buddies. The lead guitar player helped me get better. I was far from good, but decent enough to sing and play at coffee houses through college—my girlfriend singing harmonies.

"I love just to hear you pick like that," Brad said, snaking the RV around San Francisco streets on our way to Highway 1.

"Haven't played for a while. Fingers are sore. No calluses." I was curled up in the passenger seat, three-finger picking my way around an improvised selection of chords with a bluegrass feel. "This guitar…let's see…is more than twenty-five years old."

"Never played an instrument. Basketball was it, girls, and… beer," said Brad wryly.

"Guitars can get girls, you know?" I winked at Brad.

"All that touchy-feely shit, right?" Brad looked up at the big highway signs in front of us. "Is this where we turn? South, right?"

Big Sur was the next stop, and I was looking forward to the dramatic drive along coastal California Route 1. Years ago when I was in the area, the same time I visited The Haight, I was with my singing girlfriend. There's a photo tucked away somewhere in a box of the two of us standing on the rugged rocks, the ocean at our backs, splashes of foamy white water spraying behind us. We weren't posing for the camera, but instead caught in a split-second of honesty. We looked free, young, and happy. The best photos are like that, capturing the essence of the emotions, seizing a truth that would otherwise be fleeting. The old photo of my father, his dad, his grandfather and me—the one my mother stuffed away in a drawer, hoping to choke an unpleasant past—was a manipulated moment. But there was no question that snapshot of four generations of men, just like the photo of the two young lovers along the California coast, was a portrait of authenticity.

Driving on winding State Route 1 is one thing, but driving on it in a thirty-foot RV is an entirely different experience.

"You doing okay?" I asked Brad.

"You asking me or yourself?" he wondered.

"Well, it is a little hairy even from this side."

"Not exactly a piece of cake over here either."

I was watching the road markers for Bixby Canyon. It was there in Lawrence Ferlinghetti's cabin that Kerouac stayed, hoping to battle his way out of alcoholism. His time there became the basis for the novel *Big Sur*. We decided not to search out the cabin. I felt we would somehow be intruding, marching in the footsteps of all those Kerouac groupies who had come before us. Instead, I kept an eye out for the massive canyon bridge and hoped to get a look below from the high coastal road. Years later the indie band Death Cab for Cutie would write about the bridge and Kerouac, singing of a walk in the canyon and "arriving at the place where your soul had died." In that day of bright sun and soft breezes was also an awful mix of what beauty and sorrow can bring, exactly what Kerouac's *Big Sur* said to me.

"That's the bridge," I spotted it as we took a curve in the highway.

"Where the hell are we going to pull over?" said Brad.

"Are we going to stop? I gotta get a shot," said Casey, leaning against the big west-facing window in the main part of the RV. "Don't they use that bridge in some car commercials?" he asked.

"We going over that?" said Graham. "That is seriously high up."

The bridge is more than three hundred feet above the coast and runs more than seven hundred feet long. The buttresses underneath keep it from looking precarious to the driver, but there isn't a person alive who wouldn't feel a little light-headed rolling across its concrete pavement.

There was a scenic overlook just before the bridge that allowed us to park the RV and step outside. We stared at the bridge and canyon, and the ocean waves slapping the craggy coastal rocks far beneath. For several minutes, none of us said a word.

"Where's this cabin, Dad?" asked Graham softly, almost reverently.

"Down below, east of the bridge. Kerouac wrote about walking out to the water, though. Probably right down there somewhere," I said, pointing.

Graham kept his eyes on the canyon for a long time.

"Did he die there?" he asked.

"No. Died years later. But you could say he was *dying* there."

I put my arm around Graham's shoulder, both of us turning our faces toward the ocean breeze.

Casey took the last of his photos from the overlook, Brad finished up a soda he had pulled from the RV's refrigerator, and we all climbed back inside to head toward Big Sur. We were hungry and had plans to meet a girlfriend of Brad's at the Ventana Inn for lunch. The woman was someone he had met in Denver and was in California on business or for fun, I don't remember. It didn't matter. The lunch lasted four hours, the relationship only a little longer.

We stayed on the coastal highway on our way to Buellton, California. It was going to be dark when we got to our next place to sleep, arriving the same way we entered every one of the trailer parks throughout the entire trip—tired.

"Does this RV have a grill? Did we pack one?" asked Brad from the passenger seat somewhere an hour or two outside Flying Flags RV Park.

"Damn. Did we forget that?" I asked from the driver's seat, a good place for me to be, considering Brad had downed a few more glasses of wine at Ventana Inn than I had.

"Let's stop and get a grill. Buy some burgers. Cook 'em when we get to Buellton."

We found a grocery store in some small town just off the highway and bought burger patties, some buns, a bottle of red wine, and a cheap charcoal grill.

"Okay, Graham. You're going to have to put this baby together while we drive," I said.

"Me? How am I supposed to do that?" Graham asked.

"Here's a butter knife," Brad said, reaching into the small cooler we kept just behind the driver seat. "Open up the package and screw the thing together."

"With a knife?"

"You can do it," Brad said, twisting a corkscrew into the bottle of Chianti we just bought at the local store.

Graham tore the cardboard and plastic from the grill parts and attempted to set each piece in front of him on the floor just behind the cab. "I can't read the directions in the dark."

"Oh come on. Use some ingenuity," Brad said, urging him on and sipping more wine from the bottle.

That's when we heard it, a delicate metallic, *bling* and the immediate sound of something tiny rolling on the RV's floor.

"Agh!" Graham growled.

"Graham, what the hell are you doing?" Casey said from his seat at the small kitchen table.

"Screw fell."

Bling. There it was again, the same sound and the same rolling.

"I'm losing the freakin' screws!"

Graham crawled along the floor on his belly, stretching his hand out to feel along under the seats and against the RV's kitchen table legs.

"Graham, you're an idiot!" Casey said incredulously. Brad and I laughed.

"I think we are breaking a whole bunch of laws right now." Brad was amused. "Here I am with an open bottle of wine, there's a kid on the floor with no seatbelt on, and carrying a knife."

"Role models, man. Just living the dream," I said.

We made it to Flying Flags around 11:00 p.m., found our spot, hooked up the RV's water line and electricity, balanced the wobbly legs of our crippled grill against a rock, fired up the charcoal, and cooked our burgers under the stars.

"Graham, you did a fine job here, my friend," I said. "Best burgers ever on the best grill ever."

It was the first time this trip he had nothing more to say. No retorts. No snappy remarks. And that was unusual. Graham always had something to say and had been making noise since he was an infant. Even before he could speak, his first tool of communication was throwing up.

It always started with a slight, innocent cough.

Ahhak.

The second was jagged, harsh.

AhHAK.

Then several came quickly, building a strident rhythm, intensifying and crackling through the small speaker of the baby monitor on the bedside table.

Ahhak...ahHAK...AHHAK!

His mother jumped first, tossing sheets and blankets to the foot of the bed with the flip of her hand, bounding from the mattress like a night shift fireman at the first sound of the alarm.

"Here we go," Marie said, hopping to her feet, her voice muddied from sudden interrupted sleep.

The coughs turned deeper, more guttural.

BUWAAAH!

"Got the bucket?" I asked, leaping to my feet, grabbing my eyeglasses from the nightstand, and nearly tripping over the shoes discarded by the side of the bed.

"In his room." Marie answered my question nearly before I finished asking. We met simultaneously at our bedroom door practically knocking each other down.

Our son's room was directly adjacent to the master bedroom. It was the perfect second floor design for the parents of a toddler who threw up almost every night, ideal for the parents of an exploding boy.

Marie stood on the opposite side of the crib railing, positioning the blue waste bucket like a catcher's mitt, trying not to miss any of what my two-year-old son was spewing from his mouth.

The end of this throw-up routine came as quickly as it began. It was no more than a minute between the initial cough and the last discharge of projectile vomit.

"That boy can really puke," I said, stroking Graham's head to soothe him, the way any parent might. But Graham really didn't need the comforting. He never seemed distressed by these events. He never cried and never appeared irritated or anguished. He just held onto the crib railing, his chubby toddler legs wobbling. But despite how I had learned to manage these incidents and accept my son's curious patience with uncontrolled bodily reflexes, I still found it stressful to watch and struggled with the impulse to want to fix it, make it better, kiss the boo-boo.

"Can you get him a drink of water?" Marie asked, still holding the bucket close, just in case.

I stepped from the bedroom and down the hall toward the bathroom to get the black plastic cup with the image of Darth Vader emblazoned on the side.

Marie and I had every step of this drill down pat. We knew the plan of attack, and precisely how and when to act. We had perfected this unique set of actions, putting an end to the yucky consequences of inexperience: messy mattress sheets, a puke-soaked crib railing, and a vomit-saturated son.

No one could get a handle on why Graham did this. Doctors suggested it might have something to do with the respiratory ailment he had as an infant—RSV, respiratory syncytial virus. The lingering effects of the viral infection that infects the lungs and breathing passages may have made it more difficult for him to control the involuntary impulses a cough might induce.

Still, it was just a guess. It was a way for physicians to assure us that whatever caused these vomiting spells wasn't serious and Graham would eventually grow out of them.

When I was just a little older than Graham I gave my parents late night worries, too. Mine had nothing to do with coughing or vomiting, and there was no link whatsoever to illness or involuntary reactions. I simply couldn't, positively wouldn't, fall asleep.

For about a year, my father—after being nudged by my mother—would drag himself from their shared bed in the darkest part of the night, stumble into my room, lift me out of the crib, drape a blanket around me, take me outside to the driveway, and rest me on the front seat of his blue Mercury. There were no seatbelts in the cars of the 1950s, so Dad would use several blankets to tuck me in and position me as tight to the seat as possible. Then, he would drive. Anywhere. Up and down our street, around the block, to the next town, over and over. Many times it took up to an hour to get me to close my eyes. It was the repetitive road noise, the whirr of the engine mixed with the delicate, rhythmic vibration of tires on pavement that massaged me enough to finally, quietly put me to sleep. This process would work nearly every time. And when it didn't, Dad had another plan. He would bring his wide-awake son back home, plop him on the floor, and turn on the television. No cable in those days, no late night movies, no CNN, and no twenty-four-hour Nickelodeon channel. What was in front of me was the familiar black-and-white test pattern—diagonal lines emanating from a middle circle with the day's date prominently displayed along with the

David W. Berner

TV station's call letters. With this visual came the only audio available—a low, steady, unwavering tone. Change the channel and there would be another pattern just like it, each with the same dual purpose: the visual confirmation that a broadcast transmitter was active even without viewable programming, and a calibration tool for television cameras. At three o'clock in the morning, neither of these technical purposes for test patterns held any value to my father. A test pattern was there for one reason and one reason only: to hypnotize his son into dreamland.

I would hold an unwavering stare while Dad frequently reminded me, "Blink, David, blink." I didn't cry. I didn't whine or ask for a drink of water. I just sat there with my legs crossed and my eyes fixed on the screen until my head became heavy enough to convince me to change positions and lie down on the carpet. Dad would then gather a blanket around me and watch me gently fall asleep, the glow of the television casting a soft light over both of us.

Somehow, I made it through those restless nights as a toddler. Like Graham, I was uncommonly tolerant of whatever it was that was playing havoc with my young body, forcing middle-of-the-night car rides or television viewing. But my father told me those nights made him uneasy. Not long after I became a parent for the first time, my mother and father drove from their home in Pennsylvania to Chicago just a few weeks after Casey was born to see their first grandchild. One night after my mother, my wife, and Casey had gone to bed, Dad and I sat at the kitchen table over a couple of bottles of Rolling Rock beer.

156

"So, how about some advice, Grandpa," I said, jokingly.

"Oh, you'll figure it out," Dad said in his usual less-is-more approach to these kinds of discussions.

"Come on, you have to give me *something*," I said, smiling and lifting the green bottle to my mouth.

"Well, like they say, there's no manual for this stuff," he said, "but somehow you have to learn patience. That's a big one."

"Patience, huh?" I said, laughing. "You certainly got *that* down, right?" Dad had no patience. This was a guy who complained to the grocery store manager when more than two people stood in front of him in the checkout line, shouted out the window of his car to the driver in front of him if there was any split-second hesitation when the traffic light turned green, and yelled—*pick it up*—to the foursome in front of him on the golf course if they weren't keeping a breakneck pace.

"I didn't say I was good at it, just said it's important," he answered, smirking a bit. "But I do know one thing I'm good at."

"And that is?"

"Worrying."

"Worrying?"

"It's just a never-ending state of mind," he said. "It's part of the job." Dad said he worried the first time I had a diaper rash, the first time I had a cold, the first time I rode my bike alone to the corner grocery store. And he worried some more when I first learned to drive, when I went away to college, when I moved to Chicago. And he worried every one of those nights he drove me around in his car or sat me in front of the television set.

David W. Berner

"To the art of worrying," I said, clinking my beer bottle against my father's.

We took the final swigs of our Rolling Rocks.

When all had calmed down after Graham's frenetic bouts of vomiting, my son would take one last sip of water, his thick, wide hands wrapping around a sippy cup like my father's hands had wrapped around a beer. The rim of the tilted plastic glass would swallow Graham's nose and red cheeks, and his eyes would open and close in slow motion, a strong suggestion that sleep would soon take control. And after his last swallow, I would ease Graham's body to the crib mattress and pull the blanket up to his chest, sit in the white rocking chair in his darkened bedroom, and listen to his slow, steady breathing.

Chapter 14
Sweet Tarts

The morning in Buellton began with pancakes. Brad had been doing most of the cooking along the way, including making chicken tacos for lunch somewhere in Utah while I drove at seventy-five miles an hour. However, the flapjacks were made on the RV's now stationary stovetop, and we ate our breakfast and drank our coffee around a morning campfire with the vehicle's engine off and the wheels at rest.

"Where are we again?" asked Brad, slumping in a lawn chair, his fleece vest zipped to the neck to protect from the cool morning.

"Ah, we are…ah," I wiped my hand over my closed eyes, trying to brush away sleep. "We are at Flying Flags, in…ah… Buellton…ah…"

"Forget the state?" Brad asked.

Brad and I had left our sense of direction and location somewhere out on the road. There were times along the way when the whirr of the engine was a backdrop of white noise, a sound eraser that sometimes would clear our heads and other times muddy them up. This was a muddy time.

"California?" I said.

"A lot of freakin' driving," said Brad, smiling and shaking his head.

"And any *clarity* yet?"

"No fuckin' *clarity*. Foggy as ever."

The two of us laughed. The quest for *clarity* remained a running joke, even though there was truth in the search. At dozens of mileposts and along thousands of miles, Brad and I had asked each other if either had found it yet. We always said we hadn't, just to keep the gag going. But maybe we were coming closer to some sort of clarity; maybe the time to talk, think, refocus, and laugh about our search for *something* was exactly what we needed, whether we found it or not. But, if we truly hadn't yet uncovered *clarity*, we both were certain we'd better start looking a little harder if we were going to find it out here on the road.

There's something about driving a big RV along The Strip in Las Vegas that is just the epitome of tacky. But we had to do it just to say we did. Casey and Graham had never experienced Vegas, and although our visit was only a glancing blow, a drive-by with no plans to introduce the boys to a Vegas-style guys night of gambling and strip clubs, I hoped at least they'd get a taste of the spectacle. Brad wanted the two of us to sit in a couple of lawn chairs on the roof while Casey drove the RV down The Strip, but my better judgment nixed that idea.

"You know you're in Vegas when you see *that*," said Casey. He spotted the sign for the old Sahara Hotel and Casino. I don't remember if it had already been closed, but the iconic sign remained.

"This town looks like an amusement park," said Graham. "Holy crap, it's the Eiffel Tower."

"Only in America would someone put up a fake Eiffel Tower," added Casey.

"And a fake Statue of Liberty?"

"Graham, can you move a little, I want to get a photo." Casey continued to snap his way through The Strip. "I kind of thought things would be bigger, somehow."

Everything takes on a mythical grandeur when it's only a picture in your mind. Reality is never quite as impressive.

And then there's the Grand Canyon.

I had seen and done a lot of things as a journalist and believed I held a pretty healthy skepticism, allowing few things to amaze me. But like so many others who see this Wonder of the World for the first time, its vast beauty astonished me.

"Please don't tell your mother about this, okay?" I said, watching Casey climb atop a skinny vertical boulder that extended more than a dozen feet straight up. The base of the pinnacle was less than a yard wide, and the entire rock appeared to clutch the canyon's edge. Casey craved speedy, tumbling roller coasters, the faster and higher the better, and stand-ups better than sit-downs. Years later he and my sister would bungee jump and make plans to skydive. Casey was a bit of an adrenaline junkie. Although I had to smother the fear of seeing him balance against the swirling canyon wind, knees bent and arms outstretched on the rocky rim of a mile deep drop, another part of me was encouraging him to take the risk.

The four of us filled up on burgers at the canyon's lodge, preparing our bellies for the ride to Flagstaff. We drove through the Navajo Nation under a double rainbow created by a mix of sun and spotty rain, and stopped to look around at a makeshift roadside store run by Native Americans. I bought some cold cans of soda for everyone and three handmade bracelets, simple beaded jewelry, each carrying a spiritual message, I was told. One of them was fashioned of some sort of black and brown stone. The young man who sold it to me said it meant wisdom and health. My mother had been suffering from a number of chronic ailments over the last couple years, and the bracelet would make a good gift for her birthday or Christmas. I had not thought much about gifts to bring back home until now. After all, this trip was for the boys and me, not others. It didn't seem the kind of journey that prompted the buying of travel trinkets and souvenirs that would likely be forgotten in swift order. We had hoped the gifts on this trip would be of another kind. When I was a kid, even the shortest family vacations would mean at least a cheap tee-shirt or salt water taffy to carry home for a cousin or the neighbor who took in the mail. And when my mother and father traveled to England to find the boyhood home of my grandfather, my mother's dad, they returned with inexpensive fisherman sweaters and coasters with pictures of Westminster Abbey. My sons visited Abbey Road Studios with their mother on a European holiday, and their gift to me was a single white guitar pick. I loved that gift.

Sometimes the simple present is the most memorable.

It was Christmas and the boys were toddlers. My father was on his back in the middle of the living room, the twinkling colors of the holiday tree lights reflecting off the lenses of his glasses and the top of his bald head. His eyes were closed and his body motionless.

"I think we need to listen to his heart," the doctor said, placing the cold rubber end of his over-sized lime green plastic stethoscope against Dad's chest just above the pocket of his white polyester golf shirt.

"Good idea, doctor," said the second physician. "I'll check his tonsils. Open wide," he said, positioning the big baby blue wooden tongue depressor in front of my father's lips and coaxing him to unlock them.

Dad's bigger-than-average belly began to shake up and down. His chest shuddered along with his shoulders. His lips quivered. It must be hard to keep a serious face when your doctors perform emergency procedures wearing red fleece pajamas with the feet in them.

"Be still, Mr. Patient," said Casey, authoritatively. Casey was the lead doctor in this case and Graham his assistant, a duo of medical practitioners putting freshly unwrapped presents to good use. Santa had delivered each of them something called, if I remember it correctly, the *Little MD* kit. It included plastic jumbo syringes, rubber surgical scissors, and a doctor's note pad for scribbling out prescriptions for *Sweet Tarts* and *Life Savers*. I don't recall exactly, but I'm certain the doctor kits cost less than five dollars apiece.

"Mr. Patient, don't laugh. We can't operate if you're laughing," said Graham, poking the tongue depressor at my father's pursed lips determined to complete the examination even if force was necessary.

Dad was a good patient. He did what the doctors asked and promised he would be back for a follow-up appointment, a bit ironic since Dad's relationship with *real* doctors was less harmonious. He hated going to get a physical, despised checkups, and avoided both for years. Dad's excuse for not seeing a physician for over a decade: *They're always looking for something.* He was right. When Dad began having trouble urinating, the doctors went looking for something, and they found it.

I don't think the boys put those doctor toys to much use after that Christmas, moving on to bicycles and video games. In the spring, Dad began seeing an oncologist and scheduling regular chemotherapy and radiation treatments. He was with us for two more holiday seasons.

The following summer the boys' *Little MD* kits were sold at the neighborhood garage sale for fifty cents each.

Once again, it was well beyond sunset when we reached our nightly resting spot, an RV park tucked away in the desert outside Flagstaff. We stopped at a small service station and old store just off I-40 somewhere east of Seligman, Arizona, to fill up the gas tank and to buy beef jerky and a couple of cold cans of Starbuck's double espresso. The place was operated by the local Native American tribe and—along with snacks, drinks, and magazines—there were phony arrowheads and fake turquoise jewelry for sale on the counter.

"How far to Flagstaff?" I asked the man at the cash register. "Oh, it's about sixty miles," he said. "Take you about a half-hour." His calculation seemed to be utterly flawed. "But where you going?" he added.

"We're staying at the J&H RV Park."

"Oh that's a little farther. You'll get there quicker."

Graham had followed me inside and heard the exchange. I looked at Graham and tightly scrunched my face the way you do when you're certain a moment is making no possible sense.

"But if we're going around sixty miles per hour, wouldn't that put Flagstaff an hour away, and wouldn't J&H take *more* time?"

"Drive safe, now."

Graham and I widened our eyes and looked at each other, trying our best to stifle a laugh.

"Did you understand any of that?" I asked Graham as we walked to the RV's cab.

"What just happened?" Graham said, rubbing his chin.

Graham and I stepped inside the RV, and Brad turned the ignition. "What's so funny?" he asked.

"Guy says J&H is farther away than Flagstaff, so we'll get there quicker."

"What the hell are they doing in there?" Brad asked, driving the RV away from the gas tanks and to the highway. "Smoking peyote?"

I didn't want to tell him you don't smoke peyote.

We chewed the jerky, downed the cold coffees, and arrived at the trailer park in about an hour. More or less.

Chapter 15
Killing Butterflies

It appeared to be a quick, painless death. One drop of lighter fluid on the butterfly's head killed it almost immediately. The body twitched for only a second, and then in a seemingly instinctive reaction, the wings relaxed, folding delicately outward to reveal the intricate patterns and extraordinary colors that motivated me to capture it in the first place. I pierced a tiny pin into the butterfly's body and attached the insect to a piece of cardboard about the size of the wall poster found in my bedroom. I used two more pins to secure the wings, after gently pushing them open all the way so they were parallel to the body. Like the head of a twelve-point buck downed by a sportsman with a deer rifle, I displayed my trophy proudly. Butterfly catching, like deer hunting, has a distinct pattern: chase, catch, kill, and exhibit. In the summer between fifth and sixth grades, I did this over and over again. Chase, catch, kill, and exhibit. I had never killed anything before in my life, only a mosquito smashed against the skin of my arm or a lightning bug captured and forgotten inside a jelly jar. But, for a few weeks that summer, I took the life of a butterfly nearly every day.

David W. Berner

This is what you might call a flash hobby, something for which you have an intense but fleeting interest. My sons had their share of them. Casey was fascinated by the weather over one particular spring and summer. And after receiving a telescope for Christmas one year, nearly all he did for months was watch the moon. Graham was convinced he wanted to learn to shoot a bow. The arrows are now in the attic somewhere. Then there are those things we discover a passion for, even if they last only a day, that we are convinced are more important, more exhilarating than anything we have ever had an interest in before. For the boys, that was the sport of sliding on the slippery red rocks along a rushing creek in an Arizona state park. For an entire afternoon, they zipped across the soaked boulders into natural pools of water and jumped from huge stones into deep ponds. The boys wanted to know if there was a place like this in Illinois, somewhere they could regularly go to improve their new sliding skills, the way urban skateboarders seek out the best rails and concrete stairways. Many times what interests us, especially when we're kids, comes directly from the influences of others—parents, cousins, friends. But the day of rock sliding was entirely theirs; they owned it. However, getting to that place where you're making truly personal choices, even if it's as simple as what to do on a sunny afternoon in Red Rock Country, is not always easy.

When I was a kid, I lived next door to a boy who was two years older and there was nothing I wanted more than to be

168

his friend. Tom was a quiet kid. He never said much, seldom smiled, never showed his anger. Looking back, I see him as calm and cool, but Tom was also calculated. He moved deliberately through his day. Each night after dinner—exactly at 5:30 in the evening, not a minute too early or too late—he would bounce a tennis ball off the back of his house, throwing it against the concrete block foundation and catching it with his baseball glove. Tom did this for exactly one hour. He would use a gasoline mower to cut the backyard at his parent's home Tuesdays and Saturdays, and make the same precise pattern in the lawn every time. And when he took up butterfly collecting, he did it with the exactness of a scientist and the cunning of a big game hunter.

My parents thought the kid was strange, especially my father.

"That boy is going to just *go off* one of these days," Dad would say. "He's just a little too damn weird." I didn't think my father liked Tom. "Does the kid ever laugh? Does he ever talk?" Tom didn't talk much to me, so certainly he didn't talk much to my dad. But my father did know some things about Tom's family. He knew Tom didn't get along with his father, and there were rumors his dad had threatened to throw him out on the street if he didn't get straight A's in his classes at school. Tom did well in high school, and after graduation he joined the Navy and never came home again.

One summer afternoon, I sat on the stoop to the rear door of my parents' home, listening to a Pirate baseball game through the tiny speaker of my father's General Electric transistor radio. The voices of the long-time announcers had become comfortably familiar. I didn't pay much attention to the score. Instead, I was a listener-in-waiting. Every play, every inning, was simply a stepping-stone for the moment when Roberto Clemente would come to bat. Whatever Roberto did was always more interesting than whether the Pirates won or lost. I was the model of the corny character portrayed in every sappy baseball movie, the little boy wrapped up in the Gods of America's game. And Roberto was my baseball god. When I would hear Bob Prince, the Pirates' play-by-play announcer, refer to Roberto as *Bobby*, as he frequently did, I wondered with envy about what it would be like to know Roberto Clemente so well that you could call him *Bobby*.

From the stoop of my home's back door, I could see all the way across Tom's yard. Somewhere during the middle innings of one particular afternoon Pirate game, I saw Tom come out onto his porch and down the five steps. In one hand he held a small net made of tightly woven synthetic and a wooden handle. In his other was a rectangular can. It was blue and yellow, and just a bit bigger than his palm. Tom then moved quickly to the back of his yard near some hedges and opened the net as wide as it could go, holding it just off his right shoulder and above his head. With a quick *swoosh* he swung the net over the top of the bushes, and as Tom quickly moved across the yard's far south end, he did it again. He was swatting at a flickering spot of color in the air, something orange and black, floating above the hedges. I would later learn it was a Monarch butterfly.

Tom snapped his net to the ground and stepped on the handle. He grabbed a portion of the netting and held it tightly, then sat on the ground and pulled the net closer with one hand. He tipped the rectangular can, pouring something over the small section of net where a butterfly had been trapped and was now madly trying to break free. Tom waited. I waited, too. I wanted to call out his name. *Tommy, can I come see what you're doing?* But I didn't dare. Asking a question was certainly out of the question, and calling him *Tommy* would have been out-of-bounds for one of the "little kids" like me. That was the name only his teenage friends used, and I wasn't his friend. It would have been like me calling Roberto, *Bobby*.

What Tom was doing that day was something he had come to perfect: stalking a butterfly, trapping it in the net, and pouring lighter fluid on it to systemically and quickly kill it.

"Time to eat," my father said from inside the house. Dad had come home from work, and Mom had been fixing an early dinner. I stood up on the top step to the back door to get a closer look at Tom.

"Dave, let's go," Dad said from the other side of the screen door.

I kept my eyes on Tom, who was using both hands to delicately remove the dead butterfly from the netting.

"What the hell's he doing?" Dad said, looking over the top of my head toward the neighbor's backyard.

"I'm not sure," I had not seen anyone do anything like this before.

"Jesus," Dad said. "Is he catching butterflies?"

I could now see a brilliant orange color in Tom's hand.

"What?" I asked.

"Butterflies. He's catching them in the net. Looks like he's killing them, too."

"Catching butterflies?" I asked.

"It's a weird hobby. Catch them, kill them, then you show them off somehow. Never really saw anyone do it before. Figures *that* kid would be at it."

I kept watching and Dad kept talking.

"Guess it's like shooting a deer and hanging the head in your living room. Still seems weird," Dad said. "Come on. Let's eat."

The next day I asked my mother to buy me a butterfly net. It had the same white netting as Tom's, but the handle of mine was aluminum. She never asked why I was so interested in catching butterflies, although I think she knew it had something to do with Tom. Dad never said much either, until one evening he saw one of my primitive trophy displays leaning against the wall in the living room—four butterflies pinned to a piece of brown cardboard torn from an old box.

"And you're using gasoline or something to kill them?" It was clear to me that Dad was only asking this question as a way to show interest.

"Yeah, lighter fluid. You just drop a little on the head," I said. "Remember when we saw Tom do it?"

"Yeah, yeah. We saw him in the yard that day," Dad said.

"Uh, huh," I said. "And look at this one." I pointed to a Summer Azure, a white butterfly with small black dots and a gray zigzag pattern in the wings.

"Yeah, I see those around a lot," Dad said.

"Hard to catch," I said.

For a few moments my father silently inspected each of the butterflies. He carefully touched one of the wings, moving his thick calloused forefinger along its edge.

"David," Dad said. He always said *David* not Dave when he was about to make a point. This time I wasn't sure what was coming. "Do you really want to be doing this?" he asked.

"Catch butterflies?"

"*Kill* butterflies."

I had no doubts about what I was really doing. But I never thought of it as *killing* butterflies. I know that seems improbable, but the act of killing never entered my mind. I was chasing down butterflies for a very different reason, and killing them just seemed like a bi-product, a necessary thing. But now, my father was confronting me about *killing* butterflies, *me* killing butterflies. My mother never talked about killing, and she was the one who bought me the net. My friends were too busy with baseball and their bikes to question. They never said a thing. Tom didn't either. He never once talked to me about butterflies, never shared catching tips or stories about just missing a Mourning Cloak or a Red Admiral, and we certainly never talked about the beauty of flying insects or the all-too-human desire to catch and kill the things one finds magnificent.

"You have to kill them to display them," I said, hoping to justify a process that I hadn't fully understood.

"Are you doing this because Tom does it?" Dad asked.

When one of your best buddies gets a new leather baseball glove, you want one too. When your best friend gets to watch cartoons on Saturday morning TV, you want to do the same.

David W. Berner

Deep down I knew Dad was right. I *was* doing this for Tom, for Tommy. But in my young mind, I had no idea how to admit this, to process it, to understand my need to be in Tom's league.

"I'm not saying this butterfly thing is wrong, it's just that if you're going to do it, do it for *you*. Don't do it because of Tom," Dad said. "He's strange anyway."

All I could think about was what Tom would say if he knew I was going to quit.

"Years ago, I had a friend," Dad said. "He used to shoot blackbirds out of the trees with a BB gun. So, I started doing it too, until I shot a guy's pet bird right out of the sky."

"His pet?" I asked.

"A guy in the neighborhood had some black kind of bird as a pet. It got loose. It was in a tree, and I shot it. Dropped right out of the branches."

The family had a dog at the time, and I thought about how sad I would be if someone killed her. I thought about Dad with a gun, how good a shot he must have been. And I wondered if anyone could ever have a pet butterfly.

"It's not about the killing, really. It's about doing things other guys do just because you think they're somehow cool or something," Dad said. "Don't do that."

There are times when I recall what Dad said that day. It strikes me as one of those clichéd parental teaching moments, like a scene from the 1950s TV shows *Father Knows Best* or *Leave it to Beaver*. It's that scene when the dad gives the son a nugget of fatherly wisdom, taps him on the head, and sends him on his way with a new sense of direction and purpose. But real dads aren't television dads, and neither was mine. I'm

174

certain my father wasn't thinking about his role as a parent, how he could find wisdom in this moment and how he might share it with me. No, Dad saw me doing what he believed was a dumb thing to do and simply told me so.

I may have gone out again to catch butterflies a few more times after that, but I don't remember it being much fun. Many years later, after Dad and Mom were gone, I was helping my sister clean out the cellar of my parent's home, I found my old butterfly net in the storage area underneath the basement stairs. I threw it in the trash.

Brad and I sat at a picnic table and drank cans of ice tea bought from the vending machine near the park's restrooms, about one hundred yards from where the boys continued to slip and slide across the rocks.

"You look beat, my friend," I said.

"Just thinking. Wondering about this idea of culinary school and what the hell I'm going to do next."

"Just do anything."

"What do you mean by that?"

"When I went back to school to get my teaching degree, I didn't have any idea whether it was the right thing to do. But I knew I had to act somehow, do something."

"Yeah, but I still have all this other stuff hanging over my head." Brad was continuing to sort out his divorce, the selling of his restaurant, and like me, the death of his father.

"It'll work out," I said, risking sounding like an indifferent parent or a big brother. "I just think you have to make a decision, any decision. If it's not the right one, then do something else. Keep moving."

Brad swigged down the last of his ice tea.

"I don't have all the fucking right answers either, you know," I added.

Alone beside the campfire's light in the RV park that night, I looked for one of the passages in *On the Road* I had underlined more than two decades ago in my first copy of the book. I couldn't remember it exactly, but I knew it when I found it. They were the words of Dean Moriarty. He spoke of counting the miles, his worries about where to sleep, money for gas, the weather in all of its forms, and how they would be able to get to where they were going. But when it came down to it, no matter what they would face, they would end up getting there anyway.

I wanted to read this section out loud into the cool Arizona night for all of us to hear. But it was late, and my fellow travelers had gone to bed, weary from a long day under the bright, warm sun.

Chapter 16
The Politics of Fatherhood

There's a scar on Casey's face just below his left eye. When he was a crawling infant, he tugged the tail of our Golden Retriever while it slept on the tiled floor of our home's front hallway. The dog was startled and spun its body to instinctively react in the direction of the pulled tail. Its dewclaw caught Casey on the highest part of his cheekbone, cutting a deep gash. The dog was sent to live with my parents. Casey went to the hospital for stitches.

I was alone with Casey when it happened. I knew it wasn't my fault, but I was the adult in the room and that made it my responsibility. Every time I look at that scar, although it has faded with the years, I cannot help think I put it there.

Years later I took Casey and Graham sledding on a park hill. There had been a substantial snowfall over a few days, but the weather had warmed and the once soft snow on the trail had become icy, creating a wickedly fast track. When the boys were younger, I put them on the sled with me, one at a time, and rode the hill together as father and son. But they were older now, and it was time to let them go it alone or together as brothers down the hill on the long purple plastic sled. On the first run the sled wildly wobbled, flipped on its side, and was tossed into the air. The boys tumbled to the frozen track, each skidding face-first to the bottom of the hill. I took them home to their mother with faces full of jagged scratches and strawberry-colored scrapes. It was a week before the wounds healed.

We were somewhere along a desert highway just outside of Flagstaff when Graham asked about dune buggies. He wondered if there was a place we could rent a couple and zoom around the cactuses. On any other day I may have entertained the idea, but all I could think about were the scars and wounds of the past, and how a dune buggy ride might mean new wounds for the present.

We tend to believe memories are somehow relatively accessible, as easy as finding a file on a computer's hard drive or digging up an old photo in the box stored under the bed. But memories have to be liberated from our minds. They are, in essence, things we have forgotten, and it takes a bit of work to remember them. So why was I selecting to recall the memories of injury and pain? Why did I sift through my past to pull up stories of fatherly mistakes and regret? It was the residue of my afternoon conversation with Brad along I-40 not far from Winona, Arizona.

"I was not happy. Not myself. Lost. And I have no one else to blame for not doing something about it instead of retreating into my own...shit," I said, responding to Brad's questions about my divorce. I hadn't opened up to Brad about this much before. "Marie tried to help me. I wasn't ready to be helped."

It was a simple story, really. I wasn't being fulfilled in my work as a full-time journalist anymore, despite accolades and awards and a decent job. The work had soured me, and I let it destroy my sense of self. Like it or not, a man is defined by his career, and if my career was crap then I was crap. It took way too long to do something about that, and in the meantime my marriage crumbled. Going back to school helped. But the real antidote was my year of teaching middle school in one of the Chicago area's troubled school districts. It changed me.

"So, the marriage? Do you wish you could go back and do it over?" Brad asked.

"Am I sorry it happened? Yes. But I think I needed to go through this to get to where I'm headed," I said. "I'm teaching college, I'm happy again with my work, and despite the regrets, the sadness of it, I'm in a better place."

"I'm just a little behind your storyline," Brad said. "Divorce is still fresh. And work? Still trying to figure that one out."

"Give it time."

"Then there's my dad dying. A whole other thing."

"Don't I know it?"

"My dad was a good guy, but I don't want to be like him," Brad said. "He never went anywhere, never experienced life, never traveled. Oh, he was good to me. But I can't imagine living the kind of life he did."

"My father never really had a chance to grow up. Hard to do that when your dad walks out of your life when you're just a kid."

"I don't want to look back when I'm seventy and say *damn, why didn't I do that?*"

"You just don't know what *that* is yet, right?"

"I have an idea, but it still needs work."

"Some *clarity?*"

"Yep, some fucking *clarity!*"

There is nothing like a desert thunderstorm. The sky was painted with swatches of deep gray and hazy orange, a mix of thunderheads and muted sun. Lightning sparked from cloud to cloud and clouds to ground in thick spidery flashes, and the thunder exploded around us like surface-to-air missiles. Rain pummeled the RV with the intensity of a rock drummer.

"I have to get off here. I can't see a damn thing." Brad pulled into the parking lot of a deserted gas station.

Crack.

"Wooh! That was close," Casey said. Thunder and lightning appeared to be enveloping us.

Bang.

"Did you see that?" asked Graham, pointing above the roof of the abandoned service station. Lightning ignited the sky, flashing, and then hanging in the air for several seconds.

For nearly an hour we sat on this lonely stretch of highway in a gravel parking lot staring across the harsh land and the angry desert sky, flinching when the intense thunder claps vibrated our seats, and verbally applauding the light show with *oohs* and *ahhs.*

"Mother Nature was pissed," Casey said, laughing as the sky began to calm down and brighten.

"Makes you feel small, doesn't it?" Brad said.

"Insignificant," I said.

Like all of us, I had felt that way before. I was insignificant on the first day as an undergrad at a big university; insignificant as the third string trombone in the high school band; insignificant standing on the beach alone before the Atlantic Ocean; insignificant at the rocky rim of the Grand Canyon. And there was no doubt my sons had also had their moments of insignificance. It can be a good thing, humbling, and reminding us of the bigger world. But if you're not careful it can limit you. All of us want to believe we are making some sort of impact on others, making choices that will influence. I don't know if I felt that more strongly in my younger years than when I cast my very first vote. It was Jimmy Carter's initial campaign for president, and I walked around campus wearing a green and white Carter-Mondale button, proud to proclaim my decision. I kept the paper election receipt in my wallet for nearly a year. So when it was time for my first-born to vote, we were up early.

There would be times I'd play a little game with myself called Guess the Republican. It was a silly, simple game. Still, there was something satisfying about it. Standing in the long line at the polling place at the Evangelical Free Church to vote in the U.S. Presidential election of 2008 seemed the perfect place and time to play the game. And this go around, I played it with Casey, eighteen years old and voting for the first time.

Tweed sport jacket. Olive khakis. Black dress shoes with not a single scuff. Blue button down Oxford shirt. Striped silk tie.

"Republican," I whispered.

Casey shook his head, disapprovingly.

I looked down the line of early morning voters, leaning against the wall of floor-to-ceiling windows, waiting for the election commission workers to give the go ahead. Casey joked how someone might fire off a starting gun.

"What do you think?" I asked, nodding my head toward a young African-American couple standing just behind the man I had anointed a Republican.

"Oh, come on," he said. "That's easy."

"Not necessarily. He's wearing jeans, a sort of Eddie Bauer kind of shirt, and Nike running shoes. Democrat, right? But look at her." The woman wore a pair of dress pants creased to Marine perfection and what appeared to be a silk periwinkle blouse. Her hair was pulled back off her face, tight along the sides, revealing small pearl earrings.

"Dad, she's Black," Casey said. It was the morning when America was about to elect its first African-American president.

"Yeah, I know, but don't stereotype," I said.

Casey knocked his shoulder into mine, playfully hitting me. "Stereotype? Come on. What do you think you're doing with the Republicans?" he said.

London Fog-style raincoat. White pinpoint shirt. Yellow Tie. Reading emails from his Blackberry.

"Republican," I said.

"Okay, maybe, but what if he had an *iPhone?*" Casey asked, trying to trip me up.

"Then he'd be a Democrat. Republicans don't buy iPhones."

"Oh for God's sake!" Casey said.

A voice came from out of the huddle of election workers. "You can begin now."

"This is it, Casey," I said. "You are about to vote for the next president of the United States, and there's no doubt, *he's* a Democrat."

On the weekend before this Election Day, Graham campaigned for Barack Obama. He and his mother took a day-trip to Wisconsin to canvas the neighborhoods just outside Madison. They wore Barack tee-shirts freshly purchased from Urban Outfitters. The silhouette design was similar to the popular Che Guevara tee-shirts. With the shirts proudly displayed, they marched themselves up to houses to knock on doors.

"Hello, I'm volunteering for Barack Obama's campaign for change," Graham said. A young teenage girl answered the door. She had blue eyes and blonde, shoulder-length hair tucked behind her ears. She was boyish, but pretty. Graham later described her as an older "Scout" from *To Kill a Mockingbird.*

"Get the hell off my porch," the girl snapped, staring Graham down until he turned away.

"Thanks for your time," Graham said. He walked quickly down the steps to the yard, and that's where he noticed the John McCain sign planted in the side lawn, something he missed on his way up.

Graham knocked on the next door.

David W. Berner

"Yes, hello there, son." The old woman wore her gray hair in tight curls, her sweater draped over her shoulders in an effort to break the chill. She carried a cane.

"I'm volunteering for Barack Obama," Graham said, stretching his hand out to pass along red-and-blue pamphlets that outlined the politics of the Democratic candidate.

"Damn hippies," the woman said, backing up from the door and slamming it with a force not expected from elderly muscles.

"Thanks for your…" Graham's sentence was snapped in half by the clank of a deadbolt lock. "…time."

Graham's mother was working the other side of the street, and he wondered if she was having better luck. He watched her as she stood talking to a man at the entranceway to an old wood-frame home. Graham hesitated for a moment, hoping to catch her attention and get some guidance on his next move. Just then a young man in his late teens came into view from around the north corner of the street. He wore all black, his head was shaved, and he walked with a swagger. He smoked a cigarette, squeezing it with his index finger and thumb and dragging on it like a WWII soldier on a break from sentry duty. His eyes locked on Graham.

Graham tried to hide the political pamphlets behind his leg, fearing another harsh rejection and maybe, from this guy, a punch in the mouth.

"Hey," the young man muttered, slightly lifting his chin the way teenagers do to acknowledge someone.

Graham's neck tightened and his face flushed with heat.

"Where'd you get that tee-shirt?" the young man asked.

"This?" Graham asked, pointing to the face of Obama on his chest.

"Yeah, I love that fuckin' guy," the young man said.

"I don't know. My brother bought it for me."

"Gotta get one of those. Fuck McCain. My girlfriend would love that Barack shirt, too. She loves that motherfucker." The young man raised the palm of his right hand in the air, demanding a high-five from Graham.

"Yeah, I know what you mean," Graham said, smacking his hand.

"Fuck McCain," the young man said again, tossing his cigarette to the ground.

"Yeah, fuck McCain," Graham said, trying to show solidarity, fearing if he didn't things might not end so well.

The teenager became more erect as he walked past Graham, the way a young man does when he feels he's proven himself. Graham didn't think about handing him any Obama literature, but he did remind him of something.

"Don't forget to vote Tuesday."

"Yeah, damn straight, man," he said, tapping his cigarette pack and using his mouth and taut lips to slide out another smoke. "Fuck McCain," he said again, mumbling through the cigarette's filter.

Graham moved to the sidewalk and toward the next house, newly buoyed by his campaign efforts and his favorite candidate.

"Mom!" Graham yelled to his mother who was heading for another house on her side of the street. "I got a story Dad's gonna love."

David W. Berner

On Election Night, I sat down to watch the television coverage—the analysts, the numbers, the blue states outnumbering the red, the concession speech in Phoenix, and the victory speech in the lakefront air of Chicago's Grant Park.

"Ladies and gentlemen," an anonymous announcer called from the enormous speakers. "The next First Family of the United States."

Through the curtains at the back of the empty stage came the country's next president, a wife and mother, and two beautiful young girls.

"Sasha and Malia, I love you both so much, and you have earned the new puppy that's coming with us to the White House," Obama said, thanking his children for enduring the long campaign.

With everything that was happening that night, all the history, this was the moment that settled deep in my heart. We just elected this man to the most powerful position in the world, and in the middle of it all he remembered most that he was a father.

It was the campaign leading up to the election of 1972 when I found my political footing as a young man. I argued with my father about everything—the Vietnam War, protests in the streets, the Kent State shootings, the length of my hair, and George McGovern, the man I would have voted for if I had been old enough. My father was not a Republican; he was a blue-collar Democrat. But in those tumultuous times the political lines weren't drawn by party, they were mapped out by what you believed was the right thing to do in Southeast Asia, whether you believed Abbie Hoffman was a hero or a clown, whether you owned the Woodstock album. And it was also a time when the evening news broadcasts gave us a nightly illumination of the war. Night after night, Walter Cronkite would announce the body count, show us the grainy film images of bloody soldiers, and deliver bomb blasts to our living rooms through the lens of a camera. And over time, the unrelenting reporting from a steamy, blood-soaked jungle had silently and achingly chipped away at my father's hard stance on the war. I never recognized the evolution; he never once revealed the steady emotional metamorphosis. Instead, he exposed it to me unexpectedly, surprisingly, in one curt statement on a weekday evening in front of a television broadcast of the CBS Evening News.

"You're getting on a damn bus to Canada."

It was as if someone had slapped me across the face.

"Dad?"

"If this war is still going on when you have to register for the draft, I'm putting you on a damn bus to Canada," he repeated angrily.

"You'd be okay with that?"

"I'm not sending my son to some hopeless mess."

That's when Dad's politics and his fatherhood collided for the first time, when what was happening in the world was no longer just about opinion and ideology, no longer just what he read in the newspapers or watched on the nightly television news. I didn't know that then, but I know it now.

My father and I never talked again about what he said that evening, about how stunned I was. And when he voted for Nixon that fall, he still believed he was making the right choice.

But the harder decision, the one that would have put me on a Greyhound to Montreal, was one he never had to make. When I turned eighteen and registered for the military draft, the tough choice no longer had to be made. It was April 1975 when the last of the military and diplomatic staffs clambered and pushed their way out of Saigon in helicopters that hovered like hawks above a ravaged city.

In the last hours of Election Day 2008, I found myself sunk deep into the family room couch in front of the flashing colors of the late night television news broadcasts as pundits, reporters, and strategists analyzed what they had witnessed. Barack Obama had run a brilliant campaign, they said. He was a new kind of American candidate, they said. He was forging a new politics and might be the very best man for the job at one of the most troubling times in recent American history, they said.

Still, despite platitudes from talking heads, what I saw that night on that stage in Chicago's Grant Park was something different, simpler, but just as profound as the history before me. I saw a father hugging his young daughters, cheering them on to find joy in the triumphs of the night, and rewarding them with a new pet for a new home. And in the blue shadows cast by the light of the television set, I also saw the images of Casey sizing up voters at a Chicago polling place, Graham high-fiving an Obama-loving skinhead, and my father protecting me from war.

Chapter 17
Night Ride

There's a giant hole in Arizona. It's 550 feet deep and a mile across. The meteor crater hit the Southwest near Winslow some fifty thousand years ago with the impact of millions of tons of TNT. Even though it was getting dark and the visitor's center appeared to be closed, we had to stop and get a look.

"Can you see anything?" I asked, leaning out the window of the RV. Casey and Graham had walked up to a fence along the northern edge of the massive depression.

"Yeah, a little," Graham said.

"Can you imagine that hitting Earth today?" Casey asked.

"Probably knock us off our axis," Brad said.

Spinning through time in balance was terribly important, I thought. None of us want to twirl out of control, but we can't always steady our worlds or ourselves when bigger forces take over.

The drive to Albuquerque was a quiet one, each of us in our solitary thoughts. We were on the last leg of the road trip, and in some ways I was ready for it to be behind me. But in other ways I wished I could start again. Not to change anything, but to relive it. My spirit was recalculating, there was rebirth, and who doesn't want that to go on forever? Maybe each time we travel we are given a fresh canvas, a place to paint something new about ourselves, to discover or re-discover something buried in the graves of our hearts, no matter the nature of the trip. That's why five years later I would remember this silent, introspective drive through Arizona to New Mexico while on another reflective night trip, another canvas on which to paint.

I was eastbound from Chicago. The muted glow of the evening sun reflected off the rearview mirror and across the flat fields outside Bristol, Indiana. I could see towering steel irrigation sprayers lining the land, each one motionless, standing silent in nature like a giant praying mantis. John Hiatt played on the radio, and my two dogs slept in the old Land Rover's payload area. I was one hundred twenty-five miles into my travels with four hundred more to go.

The highway ran straight east to my hometown. But despite the direction I was heading that night, I was running from that place not to it, and I probably had been for years. When I was asked if I would ever move back to Pittsburgh, I always said *no, don't think so.* What once was known as Pennsylvania's steel town was no longer my true home. Still, pieces of my heart remained there alongside my mother, lying in a nursing home bed unable to walk.

I considered going to see her when she was in the hospital and then again when she was sent to a rehabilitation center.

But I didn't. And when my sister, who had lived with my mother to help care for her, struggled to deal with Mom's increasingly acerbic attitude, I also stayed in Chicago. I was working to balance my own life—a father, a college professor, and a divorced man trying to develop a new relationship with a new woman in my life.

"David, you don't know what it's like here," my sister said to me during one of many long-distance phone calls. "It's so hard."

"What's she like today?" I asked, trying subconsciously to shift the subject from my sister's deteriorating state of mind back to my mother.

"She's okay, but she cried today, and she can be an absolute bitch."

"Good thing Dad's not around. He couldn't handle the way she is," I said.

I made a similar night ride home when Dad was facing his last days, racing to beat death before it swallowed my father in his own bed in my parents' home. I arrived quickly enough to have three days and nights with him before the pain of missing my father settled in for eternity. I'm not sure he knew I was there during those last days, but I like to believe he knew. Mom sometimes thinks she sees my father lying in her bed next to her. She says she can sense him, smell him, feel his presence under the wool blanket and percale sheets. I can imagine Dad crawling into the nursing home bed with Mom, softly placing his arm over her belly, and nuzzling his chin into her neck.

Only a few car headlights illuminated the Indiana toll road. A rusty Volvo wagon passed me in the left lane, chugging

David W. Berner

its way along, the payload stacked with cardboard boxes sealed with duct tape, a rolled-up blue sleeping bag, and piles of clothes. Behind the wheel was a young man, college age. The dome light was on and a map was stretched out over the dashboard. Is he heading for a new school? A new home? Is he running *from* something or *to* it? Is he beginning a new life or ending an old one? Who is he leaving behind? Who is he going to?

When I left home for the first time, my mother and father dropped me off at the door of my dormitory on the Pennsylvania campus of Clarion State University, eighty miles from Pittsburgh on a warm Sunday night in late August of 1974. I can still see my mother wordlessly waving through the window as Dad backed out of the parking lot. She told me later that on their drive home she and my father never said a single word to each other.

I wonder if the young man in the Volvo had parents who loved him that much, who would miss him that much. I wonder if someday he too will try to balance the world he's building with the one he left behind, with an aging mother or father who inevitably will lose the battle with mobility and lucidity. I wonder if he will have to grapple with the unavoidable guilt and find himself making the same night drive I was making.

A few days before I left on this road east, my two sons asked about Nanny, the name they call my mother. Her condition had not been a secret. They had recognized she was wrestling with a number of health issues—blood pressure, arthritis, Parkinson's, and now stenosis of the spine, which forced her to be bedridden.

"Why don't we give her a call?" I asked, dialing the phone. "She would love to hear your voices."

"Hey, Nan," Graham said with his infectious enthusiasm, pacing in the kitchen, trying to walk off his impulsive natural energy.

I could hear my mother's voice coming from the phone's speaker, not clear enough to make out the exact words, but enough to detect a smile.

"I love you, too, Nanny," Graham said. "You taking care of yourself? You doing your exercises?"

I heard a little laugh from the other end of the phone.

"I'm counting on you, Nan. You got to get ready to run that marathon, you know," Graham joked. He always had a gift for lifting spirits, making people feel special and cared for. At sixteen, he talked about wanting to be a therapist or a counselor.

Casey took the phone next.

"Tell me what the physical therapists have you doing," he asked.

Again, I couldn't make out my mother's exact words, but this time the tenor of her voice had a flatter, analytical quality.

"So how many of those are you able to do?" Casey asked, like a doctor checking up on his patient. "You should set a goal, Nan. Little ones," he said. "Each goal you reach will be a victory."

Casey was showing a bit more left-brain than Graham, maybe because he was two years older or maybe because he was the first born. Casey was more likely to see the logical world, the methodical necessities of building on objectives.

"Love you too, Nan," he said, "Bunches and bunches."

Goodbyes between my sons and their Nanny had ended that way—*bunches and bunches*—since the boys began to talk.

"Is she going to die?" Graham asked as he put the phone back on its cradle. Both he and Casey anxiously looking at me for a response.

"She's strong. She has at least some of her wits about her. Her heart and brain are good. It's from the knees on down. Nothing seems to be working," I said, being honest, but still trying to soothe the worry.

My mother had always been a tough lady. She was the first feminist I knew, a homemaker with a protester's heart, a bit of Barbara Billingsley from TV's *Leave it to Beaver* weaved together with a touch of the writer and activist Gloria Steinem. When I was a boy, despite Mom's responsibilities as a traditional suburban mother and wife, it wouldn't have surprised me if she had burned her bra. She remained fiercely liberal, a supporter of Hilary Clinton's 2008 presidential campaign and in the early 1970s an intense debater at her monthly neighborhood card club gatherings, frequently speaking her mind on the issues of equal pay and a woman's right to choose, despite her Catholic upbringing. Mom was not afraid to express what she believed even when she knew those around her didn't like what they heard. She insisted the country needed a comprehensive national health care system, even though some of her friends called her a communist.

Somewhere near the border of Indiana and Ohio, I got off the highway to use the bathroom. The inside walls of the stalls were scratched with graffiti, and the pungent, sour odor of urine filled the room. The air was sticky, thick, and one of the sink faucets was stuck, spraying water in a steady stream to the drain. There was no coffee shop inside the rest stop's food court, just a no-name, all-purpose convenience store with big aluminum coffee dispensers pushed against the wall and plain white Styrofoam cups stacked beside them. I filled a cup, adding powdered non-dairy creamer and an Equal, the only sweetener left in the containers.

"One dollar, five-cents," said the portly woman at the counter with the Marlboro voice. Her stringy gray hair covered her forehead, the tops of her ears sticking out through the strands that reached to the base of her neck.

"How far to Ohio?" I asked. I had made this trip dozens of times, but still found it difficult to estimate exact time and distance.

Before she could answer, a voice came from behind me. "About twenty-five miles, honey."

She was easily seventy-five years old, maybe older. Her hair was dyed and styled into a tight coconut-white perm, her skin dotted with sunspots and wrinkles, twisting and turning across her face like roads on a map. She stood erect.

"I just came that way. Clear sailing. Good weather. No troopers," she said.

"Thanks for the heads up."

"On my way to my grandson's place near South Bend," she added, proudly. "He's back from Iraq. Haven't seen him in two years."

"That's wonderful."

The woman had a barn-full of spirit. Her eyes were bright, and she moved with mature grace and confidence as if she had never spent an idle, lazy day in her life.

"I live alone, but I like making these trips," she said, offering a bit more information than a stranger might care to hear or expect. But somehow, I didn't feel like a stranger. "Went to see my sister a couple of weeks ago in Toledo."

"You travel by yourself all the time?" I asked.

"Yep, honey, all the time. Husband died ten years ago. But, I got to keep going. Not good to sit still," she said, handing the clerk a pack of what looked to be Wrigley's gum and a dollar bill.

"Safe travels and enjoy your time with your grandson," I said.

"Safe travels to you too, young man. Again, it's about twenty-five miles, then another hour or so to Toledo."

"Got it. Have a good evening." I walked through the store, out the door, and into the night.

Leaning against my car with the window rolled down, I talked to the dogs, sipped my coffee, and watched the woman walk with a steady, deliberate stride to her white four-door sedan. It looked like a Ford Taurus. She whistled something, maybe Sinatra. I thought of my mother, how she didn't like Frank so much but loved Dean Martin and Perry Como. I thought about her at the wheel of the old family car—a dark green Pontiac Fury—and her longest solo trips, the weekly five-mile drives to the grocery store. Mom was now roughly the same age as the woman at the rest stop, but instead of driving to the store, she was lying in a steel nursing home bed, knowing she may never again make the five-hundred-mile trip to Chicago to see her grandchildren. Twenty years from now my sons will ask why their father is no longer making sense when he talks, why he can no longer bathe himself, or go to the bathroom alone. They will question why some of us move into our sixties, seventies, eighties, and even nineties with dignity, fit bodies and minds, while others never have a chance.

Somewhere near West Unity, Ohio, on a stretch of highway between Montpelier and Burlington, stillness slowly enveloped the night. The darkness engulfed nearly all that was around it—trees, farm fences, a distant church steeple. The car was quiet inside, the radio off, and the dogs asleep. I heard the steady purr of wind against moving steel and the methodical drone of tires on pavement. At that moment, like the moment I crossed into New Mexico with my best friend and my sons, the highway was empty, no one in front and no one behind.

We arrived in Albuquerque tired and hungry, and we would stay hungry longer than we had hoped.

"Our cook just quit," said the waitress. "This is going to take some time."

Not really the words you want to hear when you're sitting in a vinyl booth around a chipped Formica table inside an urban Denny's at eleven o'clock at night.

"So order something simple?" Brad said sarcastically.

"Who's doing the cooking?" I asked.

"Well, not sure yet," said the young waitress nervously, looking over her shoulder toward the kitchen. "I think our manager."

"Has he cooked anything before?" I asked.

"I think so," she said, tapping her pencil on her order pad and tucking a long strand of hair behind her right ear.

Graham snickered, and Casey put his face in his hands.

"Let's see how good this guy is. What do you think?" Brad said, challenging the restaurant staff.

"Why'd the cook quit?" I asked the waitress.

"I don't know. He just walked out."

We started with coffee, chocolate milk, water for everyone, and despite what Brad had in mind, we kept it simple: pancakes, waffles, bacon, toast.

There seem to always be stories to tell about road diners. During a college winter break, three friends and I drove to Florida from Pennsylvania. We took my car, a six-year-old Chevy Chevelle, instead of my buddy's four-wheeled wreck. No one had a lot of faith in a ride with holes in the floor, wires from a self-installed 8-track player hanging out from behind the dashboard and dangling above the gas pedal, rusted doors, and a spare that didn't fit the axle. While we were away on the ten-day trip, his parked car accumulated snow inside through a hole in the roof. A warming trend turned the snow to water, and a night freeze created a block of ice around the accelerator. We had to chip away the frozen chunk in order to get the car started. No such problems in New Mexico. The RV ran well, the air conditioning continued to churn out fresh, cool breezes, and even the trailer's shower offered uninterrupted hot water. But what these two trips did share was the diner experience.

Somewhere in deep Georgia, after driving most of the night, I pulled my Chevelle into a truck stop for breakfast. The diner was empty, except for one man wearing a John Deere hat and an ill-fitting Disney World tee-shirt that rode up above his beltless jeans, showing off a hairy back and a bulging belly. He mixed his coffee with a cigarette, a common sight in diners in those days. We took a booth in the back and waited. Five minutes. Ten. We waved and called out to the only waitress in the place, a red-haired woman in her forties with a fresh foot-long scar on her leg beginning just above the left ankle and traveling toward her knee. Several times she looked in our direction and turned away. Twenty minutes later, we left the truck stop still not knowing why we were ignored. On the drive through Northern Florida, I wondered if four hippies walking into a truck stop in Southern Georgia at 4:00 a.m. was such a good idea. I recalled some anxious moments a year before in a hunter's bar in the Allegheny Mountains of Pennsylvania. It was somewhere around midnight and the key to a cabin friends and I had rented was kept in the bar after hours. I walked in wearing torn jeans, a Crosby, Stills, and Nash tee-shirt, and denim vest with a Woodstock patch on the shoulder. My hair hung to the base of my neck and my beard hadn't been trimmed in weeks. Eyes and silence followed us through the door to the bar. Shotguns and deer rifles leaned against the walls near the tavern's tables. I felt like Peter Fonda and Dennis Hopper in *Easy Rider.*

"Is this where I get the cabin key?" I asked.

David W. Berner

The bartender, a lit Marlboro hanging from his clenched teeth, ducked behind the counter for a moment and returned with the key, handing it to me without saying a word.

He certainly must have been pleased to rent his cabin, but I don't think he would have served me a beer even if I had offered him twenty dollars for it. A trace of my old hippie spirit may have survived the years, but the days of dressing as if I had never left Woodstock were over long ago. And if there were any hippie haters in Albuquerque that night, no one would have known.

We spent nearly two hours in Denny's. I paid the bill, and we headed for an RV park on a desert bluff several miles outside and above the city. Through the darkness of the clear night, you could see the lights of Albuquerque flickering and the stars above matching every one of them.

Chapter 18
Channeling Jack

I was drawn to the simple elegance. One was made of silver, gracefully shaped with a pinhead sized turquoise stone near the top, and the other created from lapis lazuli, an intensely blue stone, the edges of the cross delicately trimmed in what appeared to be nickel. I wanted to buy one of the crosses for my nephew, but I couldn't decide. The vendor, an elderly Native American woman whose gray hair tumbled over the shoulders of her deerskin vest, sat cross-legged on the stone walkway in front of Santa Fe's Palace of the Governors with her hands outstretched, a cross in each palm. Her voice was elusive, almost fragile, as she told me how she had cut the stone and molded the metal. There was a deep shyness about her, but also a tender sense of self, a hauntingly peaceful air. The jewelry had lured me to this corner of the plaza, but she was the reason I wanted to stay.

A few months before the trip, I had been reading a number of books on Native American spirituality, after first being drawn to it years ago in my junior year of college. Who knows, maybe it was Jim Morrison who got me started. He had dabbled in it, fueled by peyote. I returned to it after the divorce, after

David W. Berner

Dad died. I was far from an expert or a faithful follower, but there was a grace about it that appealed to me. The old Pueblo woman was the embodiment of that grace, a simple internal serenity I was trying to find.

While I walked among the Native American vendors, Graham rested in the sun on a bench near the middle of the plaza, and Casey was around the corner near the San Miguel Mission with his camera. Brad was on the other side of the Plaza in front of a clothing store, pacing up and down the sidewalk as if he were guarding the place.

"Dave!" he yelled after spotting me. "Come over here."

As I walked through the grass in the Plaza's center, Brad began frantically waving his hands. "Seriously. Come on!"

"What is so desperately important?" I asked, stepping up near the store's entrance.

"There's a guy in here, says he's a Kerouac channeler."

"What?"

"Yeah, he's a Kerouac nut and believes he might be carrying around part of his spirit."

"Okay, how did you ever get into that kind of conversation with someone in a clothing store?"

Brad had been browsing around the men's section, and an employee of the store started a conversation. It began as many do between employee and customer—shirt sizes and colors and price. Brad then asked about Santa Fe and what the employee liked about living here, what drew him to this part of the country. The conversation prompted a question: why was Brad in Santa Fe's central plaza that day? It wasn't long before they talked about where we had been and this last leg of a Kerouac inspired road trip.

"Says he writes poetry like Kerouac," Brad said excitedly. "He's a little *out there*, but you have to talk to this guy."

Casey and Graham had joined us now at the storefront. Casey quickly prepared the video camera to roll on a guy who was convinced he was the conduit between Jack Kerouac in the spiritual world and the rest of us in the real world. "Oh, great," Casey said, enjoying the chance to get this encounter on tape. "A complete nut."

"Wait a minute, he thinks he's Kerouac's ghost?" Graham asked.

"Kind of like that. I know it sounds weird," Brad said. "But here we are, thousands of miles into our Kerouac trip, and we run into a guy who thinks he's walking around with his spirit? Oh come on. How could this not be fun?"

We entered the store with the camera rolling.

William Sheppard looked to be in his thirties. He wore his black hair long to his neck and sported a salt, but mostly pepper, goatee. He smiled easily, and when he saw Brad again, this time bringing along an entourage and a camera, William stepped up to meet him and eagerly outstretched his hand to shake each of ours.

"I was born in 1969, just a few days after Kerouac died," William said. "And ever since I can remember, I've been writing poetry, and I think—and I'm not kidding here—some of the poetry is Jack's."

"You think Jack's spirit is writing your words?" I asked.

David W. Berner

"I absolutely swear it's true. And I've been to Kerouac's house in St. Petersburg, the last place he lived before he died."

"Yeah?"

"Threw up in the yard. Drunk as hell. Maybe a little like Jack, huh?"

Casey took his eye away from the camera and glanced at me, mouthing: *The guy is loony.*

"So why Kerouac?" I asked.

"I'm a free spirit. Feel like I should have been around in the '50s reading poetry in smoky bars. Wish I would have been eighteen years old in the Summer of Love."

I didn't want to tell him he was mixing two different generations, youth cultures. But I think he was smart enough to believe what so many others did: Kerouac may not have been a hippie, but he opened the door for them.

"I've done the road trip thing, too," William said. "Had a lot of epiphanies out there. You can learn a lot about yourself on the road." He paused, appearing for a moment to relive one of those intuitive leaps in understanding. "Been to the East Coast, West Coast, and went to Mexico once, some old world spot. There was a bazaar or something going on. Some guy tried to kill me with a pool cue. His girlfriend kept winking at me. He didn't like that much," he said, highlighting only the story's main points, as if there were details he wasn't ready to reveal to just anyone. "I want to go to Lowell someday, too."

Kerouac's hometown in Massachusetts was a working class city when he grew up there, and still is today. There's a park named after him. Kerouac is buried in Edson Cemetery. Carved on the simple gravestone: "He honored his life." Visitors leave flowers and bottles of wine.

"Ever see that famous picture of Dylan and Allen Ginsberg at Kerouac's grave?" I asked.

"Yeah, I got some book with that in it. I want to be there. Maybe I'll get some confirmation on this connection I have. Find out whether I'm really channeling Jack."

A confirmation was unnecessary. If this guy believed he was carrying around Kerouac's spirit, then he should simply, emphatically, embrace it. Make it his, write his poems, drink a few for Jack, and go on the road.

"You should do it," said Brad. "Head for Lowell."

"Yeah, I am certainly going to do that someday. Yep, I think I will," he said, seemingly confirming now the itinerary for a trip considered many times before.

We talked about our favorite Kerouac books. William was definitely a fan of *The Dharma Bums,* but in the end nothing beat *On the Road.* And what about the poetry? I liked Kerouac's haikus and mentioned a favorite about a businessman walking alone near a football field. William's favorite was *San Francisco Blues,* a collection of poems and quoted a couple of lines. "And *The Book of Blues* just blows me away," he said. We talked about the grainy black-and-white YouTube video of Kerouac's night on *The Steve Allen Show* just after *On the Road* was published, and how Kerouac appeared uneasy and anxious with a sweaty brow and an unnatural manner.

"Did you ever see the last TV appearance in the late '60s?" I asked.

"He's with William F. Buckley, and he's drunk out of his mind," said William.

We both agreed it was sad and painful to watch.

"He was the spokesman for a generation, but not the hippies. He hated that idea," William added.

I asked if he had read the recent news stories about how the *On the Road* scroll, the original manuscript, would soon go on display around the country.

"Wherever it is, I'll be there," he said.

In May of the next year, the scroll came to Santa Fe for a month-long exhibition, displayed under glass and guarded by twenty-four-hour security. More than eight hundred people came to see it on opening night inside the Palace of the Governors just across the plaza from the clothing store where William Sheppard helped tourists find the correct shirt size, choose the right turquoise-studded belt, and he would often use his breaks to slip away to craft words in a notebook he carried in his pocket, a notebook full of poems.

In *On the Road,* Kerouac wrote about the "moment when you know all and everything is decided forever." Wouldn't it be wonderful if there were such a moment? Truth is, even Kerouac and his character Sal Paradise admitted that finding that moment was unlikely, even impossible. Although Santa Fe was beginning to feel like a place where I might be able to uncover a little of what Sal and Dean called *it*, discover some tiny answer to the big questions about the life before me and my role as a man and father, I knew this was only my heart talking and not my head.

Like Kerouac's characters, I wasn't going to find *it* on the streets of Denver, in the unearthly beauty of Moab, inside City Lights Bookstore, at the Bixby Canyon Bridge, under the rainbows in the Navajo Nation, on the edge of the Grand Canyon, in Santa Fe, or back in Chicago. But maybe I could come close. Maybe somewhere in the deepness of my soul there was a place, a dark cavity that held the Holy Grail of consciousness. Maybe the long journey we all take alone in this world is *it*. Not just this trip or any single trip, but instead in the vast meandering travels of life, all those physical and emotional journeys our fathers have taken before us and the ones we will take in our futures, combining to create one dashboard road map, a step toward something timeless. Maybe *it* is the map, all those highways calling on each of us to either stay in motion or be lost in the sadness and hardships of life. Maybe that's what Kerouac meant when he wrote about feeling like death was on his heels, compelling him to keep moving. Maybe William Sheppard was onto something. Whether we believed he was channeling Kerouac or not simply didn't matter. William believed it, and that made it his truth, his road on a personal journey to find the elusive *it*.

We had dinner on a restaurant's balcony overlooking the Plaza. Brad and I shared a bottle of wine, and the boys drank Cokes and ate quesadillas. None of us wanted to leave Santa Fe without something to remember our time here, a little piece of this sacred place that left us with an indescribable yet mysterious impression far unlike other mileposts. Casey bought a piece of Native American pottery made from clay and horsehair, and

David W. Berner

Graham was drawn to a silver Hopi Indian necklace with the Kokopelli symbol on it, an icon of good luck and fortune. I purchased the crosses for my nephew and a book on Native American spirituality. And Brad bought a mirror, a large looking glass framed in distressed Arizona cypress. Although it seemed a hopeless cliché, the symbolism could not be missed.

"Do you find it weird that you were drawn to a four-foot mirror, of all things?" I asked Brad. "You're trying to figure out who you're going to be in the next chapter of your life, and you buy a mirror?"

"Looking right at myself, aren't I?" said Brad. "Right there in the reflection—every bit of me—good, bad, and ugly."

"Not a piece of art, not some book, or bottle of wine. You buy a mirror."

"I saw it and had to have it. It's like I was...compelled."

"Strange to you?"

"Yeah. I don't go around buying mirrors much," Brad said.

"Maybe it's time."

"Yeah, maybe it's time."

We decided to head north to Denver that evening. The forecast called for heavy storms moving west to east across northbound I-25, but none would hamper our travels. Instead, they were a welcome distraction from the long four-hundred-mile drive in front of us. The weather ushered in a watercolor mural above the high desert, painting tequila orange and deep blue across the late-day sky, and blowing in billowing charcoal clouds saturated with moisture, each taking turns bursting rain drops on the windshield.

Chapter 19
Lost and Found in Missouri

Four years after our cross-country drive, I was on a different kind of trip. Somewhere in the flat, horizontal land of central Missouri, between the farm towns of Vandalia and Laddonia, I was on the phone with Brad, trying to convince him that the risks he had taken were good ones. I said this like I knew what I was talking about.

"You got to have something to lose to make it worth it," I said, paraphrasing the lyrics of a Foo Fighter's song. Brad and I had been on the phone for nearly an hour, and our entire conversation had centered around one daunting question: what he was going to do with the rest of his life? About a year after our cross-country trip, Brad put all his efforts and money into a new business, a venture involving organic foods with a plan to distribute to Colorado schools. The idea had promise, Brad was receiving moral support, but instead, the plan went disastrously wrong, forcing him to max out his credit cards, deplete his savings, and move out of his Denver condo and in with a friend in the suburbs. Bankruptcy seemed the only option.

"What? No Dylan?" Brad laughed, after hearing me reference the Foo Fighter's lyric.

"Oh, sooner or later I'll quote Dylan, I'm sure," I said, echoing his laugh. Referencing Dylan, Lennon, Hemingway, of course Kerouac, and an occasional contemporary musician or writer was something I did often, a habit some found annoying, including my sons.

"It's about taking it to the limit," I said. "You have to be willing to let it all go, lose something, maybe everything. That's what makes risk-taking what it's supposed to be."

"I certainly risked it, didn't I?" Brad said. "And isn't that the Eagles?" He was trying to trip me up with the reference to "taking it to the limit." I ignored him.

"And that, my friend, in the big scheme of things is a good thing, isn't it? Risking it."

That was easy for me to say. I wasn't seeing my financial world crash and burn around me.

Miles ahead in Columbia, Casey was in a dormitory at the University of Missouri, packing up to come home for the summer. In order to get everything he rat-packed during his freshman year back to his home in Illinois, we needed his car and mine. There was plenty to truck home: a silver toaster, plastic cups and plates, a bicycle and a bicycle helmet still in store packaging, a lime green oval folding chair purchased at the local Walmart, and plastic crates and cardboard boxes overflowing with computer wires, belts, coffee mugs, an extension cord, and two jumbo bags of M&Ms.

Packing and moving were sensitive subjects to bring up with Brad, so I was careful not to get into too much detail about all the work it would be to get Casey and his belongings back home. I didn't even want to talk about having to use two cars. Just a few days before, the bank had threatened to repossess Brad's Audi.

"It's hard. I don't want to make another wrong move," Brad continued. "I've already made one."

There was something positive here. Brad had a clean slate in front of him, few remaining ties to Denver, and could go anywhere he wanted to start fresh. Like Casey, he too could bundle-up his life and move on to a summer of new beginnings. But it wasn't that simple.

"Look," I said, "I may be full of crap, and I certainly have never been where you are, so what the fuck do I know, but if you worry too much about making the right decision, about the next thing, you'll be stuck. You'll run in place."

"Yeah, I think I'm resisting the inevitable," Brad said.

I wasn't sure I knew exactly what he meant, but I saw no other alternative. He needed to make a move, any move. He needed to just *get going*.

"Here. How's this?" I said. I took a breath and referenced Dylan's lyrics from the song "Mississippi." "Dylan says you got to keep moving, and everyone is moving if you haven't already arrived, right? Everyone has to keep moving if they're not satisfied with where they are at that moment."

There was a confusing intersection of highways near Laddonia, and I wasn't sure I would remember which turn to make, the best route to Columbia. Last time, I attempted to knock off some time and miles and drove straight through the crossroads instead of making a left. I was lost for nearly an hour.

"Hey man, I got to run. Not sure where I'm headed here," I said guiltily. I had to cut the conversation short. "Let's talk in a few days." Before hanging up the phone, I suggested he come to Chicago, decompress with his buddy, and forget about things for a while. It was a long time before he did that.

I pulled the car off the road, pressed the map application on my iPhone to check the directions again, and then called Casey.

"I should be there in about an hour or so," I said.

"Where are you?"

"Somewhere in the middle of Missouri."

"Well, yeah. I kind of got that. *I'm* in the middle of Missouri, too," Casey said, mocking his father's attempt at humor.

So many of my phone conversations with Casey went like this one. He wasn't much for frivolous discussion or meaningless banter. When he was in elementary school, I used to call him my *little man* because of his sober, analytical nature. He was a corporate executive in a Star Wars tee-shirt. But he was also intuitive, thoughtful, introspective, and his mind was always considering the possibilities. When Casey was seven years old, he sold printed-out weather forecasts to the neighbors. He searched the Internet, personalized the forecasts for our town, and printed and pitched the benefits of his predictions door-to-door. He made a few dollars every couple of days. Those early entrepreneurial endeavors were born out of a calculated, restrained, and determined personality. But changes were taking place. At nineteen years old, Casey was uncovering other sides of his character, widening his arms for a bigger hug of the world. He wasn't ready to share openly all of what he was discovering, but it was all there in the shade of his bigger self.

I hung up the phone with Casey, and thought of another Dylan lyric. It's from the song "My Back Pages." *I was so much older then. I'm younger than that now.*

Casey's fourth-floor dorm room was the last on the north end of the hallway. Hand-drawn, crayon-colored cutouts of his name and that of his roommate were still taped to the wall outside his room. They had been there since the first day of classes.

"The guy's a pig," Casey said, opening the door.

Heaps of clothes filled the room—mounds of neglected tee-shirts, jeans, and underwear. The patterned entrance rug with the geometric colored shapes, purchased just before he moved in was faded from months of accumulated dust. A box of opened Wheat Thins sat on top of the small refrigerator, crumbs scattered at the box's base.

"I can see that," I said, looking around the room. "Are these clothes all his?"

"Only one pile is mine," Casey said defensively, pointing to a heap near the door. He nodded his head toward cardboard boxes packed with assorted papers, books, a radio, and a small lamp. "It all goes. That. That. And this," he said, tapping his hand on a portable humidifier.

"Have you used it?" I asked.

"Oh, yeah. The other night when I had some sniffles? Big help."

During this freshman year, Casey and I didn't talk as often as he and his mother talked. There was a weekly phone call, an occasional email, and a Skype call or two when he and I took the time to plan for it. His busy school schedule and the hundreds of miles between us created a father-son obstacle course. It took deliberate maneuvering, a few hurdles to jump to make a connection. We both tried, but neither of us tried as hard as we could. He defaulted to his world at Missouri. I defaulted to my life in Chicago. No excuses. It was just what happened. But now, among the clutter of his belongings, I realized how much I had missed him.

We spent an hour packing the cars, rolling dolly after dolly of piled-high possessions from the dorm elevator to the parking lot. Other parents and their children were doing the same, interrupted only by family members or friends saying hello or goodbye with a handshake, hug, or kiss.

"Is that it?" I asked, looking over the inside of the two cars, bulging with a school year's worth of freshman souvenirs.

"I think we're good," Casey said, wiping his sweaty forehead.

"Let's get some food. I'm starving." I opened the door to Casey's car and climbed in the passenger side. "Take me to your favorite place. I'm buying."

Nine months ago in this same parking lot on a hot August day, Casey's mother and I spent hours unloading our son's life into the same elevator and up to the same tiny dorm room he was now leaving behind. We had a dinner of fish and pork chops at one of the nicer Columbia restaurants, and celebrated with chocolate cake for dessert. The three of us stood on the sidewalk in front of the dorm and hugged. And as the sun fell behind the trees and the campus buildings, his mother and I watched Casey walk away. He never turned around for another glimpse or a final wave goodbye, a promise he'd made to himself, and disappeared through the glass doors of the dormitory and into the mix of students and the shadows of the lobby. On the drive back home, his mother cried, and hours passed before I said a word.

"I have just the place," Casey said, responding to my call for food. He opened the car's driver side door and tossed his keys in the air, catching them in his other hand. "The Berg."

The Heidelberg was a familiar restaurant and bar, the kind found in hundreds of college towns. At one of the long tables, giggling sorority girls—made-up for the night—ordered burgers and salads. At a small table near the bar, a mother and father sat silently with their teenage son. Three college boys drank from bottles of Pabst Blue Ribbon at a table next to the stairs that led to rooftop seating. Casey walked quickly through the main dining area and up the creaky steps.

"This is where the homecoming committee goes all the time after meetings," he said over this shoulder. Casey was selected for the committee in his second semester. "But I think the meetings are just an excuse so we can come here," he added, smiling.

Casey knew exactly where he was going, moving directly toward the table near the railing that overlooked the university's journalism school. He said hello to the waitress, someone he had seen many times before, and waved off the menu. He knew what was on it.

"I've got something to tell you," Casey said. I glanced up from the menu's list of beers on tap and leaned back in my chair. "I've been eating a little meat," he said.

"Really?" I was surprised. Casey had been a vegetarian for several years, eating only fish now and then.

"Yeah, I just think it's time to get some more meaty protein in my life. Just a burger now and then," he said. "We'll see how it goes."

Casey had plans to stay on campus a few days longer to tie-up some matters regarding work he was doing for the school's alumni association, and figured he'd have one more chance for a burger at The Berg. He was moving off campus in the fall and might not frequent the restaurant as often. Renting an apartment seemed a bold decision. But it really wasn't. It was the same kind of decision Casey had made many times before. In eighth grade, he initiated a project of documenting his class by taking photos and presenting a produced video to his classmates and their parents at middle school graduation. His teachers asked him to give a speech at the ceremony. He accepted without hesitation. In high school, he produced The Senior Video, a photographic memory for students and their families. There was the student ambassador trip to Australia and New Zealand, and the trip to Iowa to help produce a student documentary on the National Guard's efforts to aid flood victims. Some might see this as one parent's insufferable list of a child's accomplishments. But each of these decisions was Casey's, not his mother's and not mine. And in every situation, both in big and small ways, Casey was simply taking his own kind of risk. Even the choice to eat meat again, a seemingly immaterial decision, was one of those risks. And in each of these choices there was something to lose, making the decision worth the anxiety, stress, and apprehension.

"It appears you've thought a lot about this meat thing," I said.

"Yeah. Interesting to see how my body reacts after not eating any beef for so long. I don't think I'm going to start throwing up or anything," Casey said, chuckling. "No worries."

It was a starlit night when I began my trip back from Missouri to Chicago, quite unlike the changeable and sometimes unsettled skies above Brad, the boys, and me on the drive north from Santa Fe to Denver. These were different roads for different times. But for stretches along both I-25 past Valmora and Wagon Mound in New Mexico and Route 54 near Auxvasse and Vandiver in Missouri, the rural darkness was similarly startling, as if someone had put their heavy hands over my eyes. No streetlights, not a shining lamp in a Missouri farmhouse or New Mexico ranch, only an occasional set of headlights beaming from the opposite direction. Although I was not alone on the northbound drive through New Mexico as I was on the trip from Missouri, I still found myself seeking out a lonely, singular place on that road to Denver, wondering silently if this cross-country tour, now almost complete, had been anything more than a diversion. I believed in the power of the road. I believed journeys could be healing, ointment on wounds. And I believed they could present promise, new insight, and yes, even clarity. I had hoped the Kerouac trip would somehow allow me to see my father as I never had, and tame the insecurities I harbored about my role as a dad. But it was becoming increasingly clear on the drive through Northern New Mexico and into Southern Colorado that this five-thousand-mile trip wasn't going to accomplish all I wanted it to, not all by itself. It would take the passage of time, this trip and others—more voyages of the soul and spirit—to get me where I wanted to go.

"There's that line at the end of *On the Road*," I said to Brad somewhere near Pueblo, Colorado. "It's sad, but true."

"Haven't read it yet, you know?" Brad said, grinning.

"Yeah, I know. Promise me you will someday, okay?" I asked. "And when you do, spend some time on those final paragraphs, read them slowly. The line I'm talking about is right there on the last page. It's about discovering that the only thing we really know about what's going to happen to us in this life is that we're all going to grow old and die."

"Uplifting."

"But if you know that truth, believe in it, accept it, isn't it somehow comforting? Maybe even liberating? "

Brad smiled and turned to look out the passenger side window as soundless lightning streaks, like fingers of a hand, stretched across the black sky and vanished on the horizon.

On the drive home from Casey's school, not far from the bridge that crosses the Mississippi at the Illinois-Missouri line, I pulled the car on the gravel at the side of the road. The boxes, books, and plastic crates crammed in the hatchback and backseat shifted and rubbed against the vinyl interior, creating that familiar squeaking sound of unsecured belongings. But when the car came to a stop, everything fell silent. I looked at the display on my phone: 11:03 p.m. I thought about phoning Brad to see if he thought any more about what we talked about.

I considered calling Casey to say goodnight one last time. I did neither. Instead, I turned off the phone, rested it on my lap, placed my hands behind my head, and sat motionless in the dark, thinking of all the risks yet to be taken and all the precious things I would never want to lose.

Chapter 20
Fixing a Toilet from Heaven

There was a lot of wine in Denver, and Brad and I drank glass after glass as we sat on the deck of his apartment in the afternoon sun.

"When you're trying to figure out the rest of your life, you just have to start somewhere," Brad said. "Just like the road trip."

"And end somewhere, too. Do you feel sad it's over?" I asked, reaching for the bottle of white table wine.

"It does seem strange not to be in motion."

"We're both still in motion, my friend. We are definitely still in motion."

"The body is still, the mind is racing," Brad said. "But I feel something...I don't know...a *newness*, don't you think?"

"Tired, but recharged?"

"Yeah. Take what you got from the road and carry it with you."

The boys and I had a two-day drive back to Chicago in front of us, but no one was in a hurry to get going. Home meant the boys would be closer to returning to school, and

221

David W. Berner

I would have to start preparations for a full load of classes to teach at the college and a long overdue trip to Pittsburgh to see my ailing mother. But for now, a lazy day in Denver was a better idea.

"How about a toast?" said Brad, lifting his glass. "Casey and Graham, grab something to drink."

Graham reached for the wine.

"Go ahead," Brad said. "Uncle Brad won't mind."

"Ah, how about a Pepsi?" I stole the bottle from Graham's hands.

"To the road," said Brad.

The two of us clinked our glasses of wine and against the boys' soda cans.

"To Kerouac," I said.

"To clarity!" said Casey.

We ordered pizzas, Brad and I watched the Rockies baseball game on television, and the boys sunk into a movie on Casey's computer. There was no more talk that night about the trip, no more introspective conversations, no more Kerouac quotes, no more discussion about divorces, jobs, or fathers and sons. The days on the road and what they would mean, signify, or promise would eventually be processed, but not by way of quickie, drive-thru pseudo-analysis. What the trip had stamped on our souls would reveal itself in time, in a quiet early morning alone in the back corner of a sleepy coffee shop, on a packed Friday evening commuter train out of Chicago, at dinner with a lover, at the grocery store, in the shower, sweeping the floor, planting impatiens, raking leaves, folding laundry, washing the dog. It would come in tiny pieces, unexpected awakenings,

222

memories mixed with dreams. This was not only true for Brad and me, but maybe especially for the boys. Our traveling copy of *On the Road* was with us for every one of the five thousand miles, on the dashboard like one of those stick-on compasses or St. Anthony statues. Casey and Graham never picked it up. Never read a word. But because of this trip, someday they will. Someday they'll study Kerouac's words and imagine what their father saw when he looked out the RV's windshield and into his heart.

Two months after the trip, I sat in a chair at my mother's bedside in the nursing home in Pittsburgh. Mom appeared troubled. Her eyes were bulging and buggy, the skin on her face translucent and gray.

"Is she pregnant?" Mom whispered the way one does when a secret is about to be revealed.

"No," I whispered back. "Diane is not pregnant, Mom."

My mother was absorbed in the false belief that my sister was going to have a baby, and that it was a shameful secret. Nurses said this recent delusion was a product of her illness.

"Well, someone told me in a note inside a Christmas card. It was written in very small print and hard to read. They said she was pregnant. And the father?" she said, pausing to be certain we were alone. "The father is a Black man."

"No pregnancy, Mom. No Black man," I said, attempting to be patient with her. My mother had plenty of wild stories to tell, emanating from the deep and mixed-up recesses of her mind. She shared these stories with anyone who would listen, each an odd blend of old and new memories, rambling opinion, pieces of nonsense, and bizarre secrets. Some would carry a shade of truth, but not much logic.

Diane had never wanted children, had shunned any talk of marriage since her teenage years. And at forty-six years old, my sister did not appear interested in any sort of relationship with any man of any color, ethnicity, or religion. You might say she was taking a break. You might say she was far too set in her ways. You might say she had nothing left in her emotional reservoir for a relationship with a man, not after caring for my ailing mother for three years, helping her in and out of bed, sponge-bathing her, feeding her medicine, and staring at late night TV from the chair next to the bed while my mother fell asleep.

Mixed with Mom's stories were moments of lucidity, periods of silence, and peculiar arthritic hand gestures. Her spinal stenosis had worsened, she was fighting congestive heart failure, high blood pressure, diabetes, and breathing problems related to her battle with tuberculosis as a young woman. She was diagnosed in 1954, just months after marrying my father and quarantined for 18 months in a sanatorium. Every doctor there believed she was going to die.

"Dad was here today," Mom said. She had been talking a lot lately about my father.

"He was, huh," I said.

"He was working on something in the bathroom. Fixing the toilet."

My father was a compulsive handyman. When he was healthy, no one could stop him from repairing, renovating, tweaking anything and everything in my parents' home—door locks, kitchen cabinet hinges, light fixtures, thermostats, gutters. It seemed perfectly natural that his ghost would have been in my mother's room that day adjusting the float on the commode.

"He never talks to me, though," Mom said sadly.

"Never?"

"Nope. He did wave to me once," she said, looking away into an empty space in the room.

"What does Dad look like when you see him?" I asked.

"Like he did when he died. Gray and thin. And he wears his uniform."

My father's last job was a carpenter, a maintenance man at the downtown Hyatt hotel in Pittsburgh. He wore the company's standard uniform: navy blue flat front pants, a light blue shirt with dark blue collar. His first name was embroidered on the left chest. It took Dad a long time to get used to the public display of his name.

When Bill Clinton was running for President for his first term, he came to Pittsburgh to campaign and made his way into the Hyatt. My father loved to tell the story of how Clinton burst into the lobby, filling the room with his presence and immediately began shaking hands. Reporters, aides, and campaign workers swirled around Clinton as he made his way to the hotel's front desk. He smiled at the clerks at the reception desk. My father stood near the decorative water fountain in the middle of the lobby, watching quietly. Dad was skeptical of politicians; he had a natural contempt for them. And even though he was a lifelong Democrat, at this point he wasn't sold on any candidate, including Bill Clinton.

Dad watched as Clinton mingled with guests, stopping to talk to hotel employees who were now clamoring around him. But somehow, Clinton must have noticed my father's reticence. Dad said he stood with his hands in his pockets, his work boots firmly planted on the lobby's ceramic floor, and observed as Clinton shook hand after hand.

"How are you? I'm Bill Clinton and I'm running for President," Clinton said in the same throaty crackle impersonators would later imitate on late night TV shows.

"Good to meet you, Mr. Clinton," my father said. He extended his strong hand and locked it around the candidate's. "Got one question for you, though." When Dad told this story—and he did many times—it was here that the tenor of his voice shifted, sounding as it did when he'd question whether I had mowed the lawn, knowing full well I hadn't. "Are you going to do everything you say you will?" Dad asked.

"I'm going to try, Norm. I'm certainly going to try."

Norm?

My father was uncharacteristically silenced.

How did he know my name?

Clinton tapped my father's shoulder, removed his right hand from Dad's grip, and turned to another hotel employee, a manager who had positioned himself to the candidate's left. As my father watched Clinton move through the far end of the lobby and out of sight, Dad reached his right hand to the chest of his shirt and ran his fingers over the threads that spelled out his name. He smiled as if he had solved a riddle.

That uniform with the embroidered name was what my mother saw my father wearing whenever he visited her room.

"Why do you think he's wearing his uniform, Mom?" I asked.

"I guess he thinks he has things to do. There's work to be done," she said.

That's how many people, including my mother, saw my father—the handyman who enthusiastically accepted the responsibility to repair whatever household item needed it. Still, I couldn't help but wonder if some of the *work to be done* wasn't more than that. My father had always been the fix-it guy, the workingman with the talented hands. It was a part of his identity, and fixing what was broken was Dad's way of showing love. Maybe my father's ghost—the one my mother believed frequently visited her—came down from Heaven not only to show he still dearly loved my mother and to repair a drippy faucet, wallpaper the kitchen, or fix a toilet, but also to continue the work that would heal the sins of his father, his most important fix-up job. I was certain Dad was never able to fully confront the emptiness he experienced as a young teenager when his father walked away from his mother and out of his life. As a consequence, he became a cautious and protective father, obsessively omnipresent. Somehow he believed the bond with his son would never be broken if he was always *right there,* all the time. Dad knew the pain of being fatherless, and believed that if he had anything to do with it, his son would never be without his dad. Maybe *this* was the *work to be done.* Maybe my mother's visions of Dad were reminders that the job of a being a man and a father has no limits and no end, just like all good and meaningful road trips. And maybe Dad was with us along every mile of that cross-country journey, always at the ready in case something needed repairing—the RV or our spirits. Maybe soon, Dad would appear before me, hand me a metaphorical hammer, and demand that I not only continue the good work of the fathers who came before me, but forgive their failures and my own.

Mom became quiet and closed her eyes. I massaged her hand and could feel each bone, taut tendons, and rubbery veins. The skin on her hands was still remarkably soft and velvety, like the silk of an expensive tie. When she was home, she kept bottles of Jergen's hand moisturizer at the kitchen sink and on her nightstand. She'd squirt the thick, milky liquid into her palms, rub her hands together, and deposit the excess on her cheeks and neck. No one else used the moisturizer in our house, certainly not my father. He was of the generation who believed lubricants were to be applied to machinery not to men. I wondered what it must have been like for my mother to hold my father's hand—his thick fingers, the scaly calluses near his knuckles, and the coarse, dry skin. Dad would sometimes use gasoline to clean up after completing a particularly messy chore, working the corrosive liquid deep into the skin. His hands were clean but rough, not exactly what a woman might want on her shoulder, waist, or lotion-softened palms and fingers. Still, I don't ever remember my mother complaining about my father's touch. Silently, she may have wished he had touched her more often.

"Diane doesn't believe I see your dad, you know." Mom leaned slightly toward me. "Your sister thinks I'm crazy," she whispered.

"Mom, if you see Dad, then that's what you see. It's your reality," I said.

"Do you see him?"

"No, I don't Mom. But that's okay."

My mother turned her eyes away from mine and pulled her lips inward, almost biting them, the way one does when contemplating something difficult to say.

"I know you all think I'm seeing things," she said. "But I'm not loopy."

"You are not loopy, Mom."

"Your dad is waiting for me, you know. He hasn't crossed over yet, and he knows I don't have much time left."

"You think that's why he's not saying anything?"

"He can't. Not until I am ready to go." Mom's lips quivered.

"How do you feel about that?" I softly asked. "Are you scared?"

"No. Not at all." Her voice had been weakened and deepened by age and illness, but for just a moment the vocal frailty disappeared. "I'm kind of looking forward to what's to come. Maybe I'll get some answers to the mysteries, huh?"

"That would be something, wouldn't it?" I said, holding her hands.

Mom lifted her head from the bed's pillow, arched her eyebrows, and stared into my eyes as if trying to will me closer. "Your sister, when she's fixing something in the house, something Norm would have done, she can only do it properly because Dad's spirit is beside her. I can see him. But when I die, because Diane doesn't believe in all that ghost stuff, Dad won't be there for her anymore, and she'll lose all of her handyman abilities." Then, like an unspoken exclamation point, Mom gave a little nod and said, "It will just...simply...vanish."

My mother returned her head to the pillow. She closed her eyes, and I watched her rest for a several minutes.

"A nap would be a good thing, Mom." I placed her hands together on her belly just below her breasts.

"Diane won't be able to fix a single thing," she whispered, her eyes remaining shut. "Poof. All gone."

I tucked the edges of Mom's bed sheet around her legs and waist, turned off the lamp beside her bed, sank into my chair, relaxed my head against the seat's high back, and closed my eyes, wondering if Dad was somewhere near watching us rest.

About the Author

David W. Berner is a journalist, broadcaster, writer, and teacher. His first book, *Accidental Lessons* was awarded the Royal Dragonfly Grand Prize for Literature. His stories have been published in a number of literary magazines and journals, and his broadcast reporting and audio documentaries have aired on the CBS Radio Network and dozens of public radio stations across America. Chicago is his home.

About Dream of Things

Dream of Things (dreamofthings.com) publishes memoirs, anthologies of creative nonfiction, and other books that fulfill our mission to publish distinctive voices and meaningful books. Other books from Dream of Things include:

She's Not Herself
A Psychotherapist's Journey Into and Beyond Her Mother's Mental Illness by Linda Appleman Shapiro
"An honest and compelling story by a brave and gifted writer."
Wally Lamb

Betty's Child
A Memoir by Donald R. Dempsey
A Hoffer Award Grand Prize Finalist.
"Heartrending and humorous." *Kirkus Review*

Swimming with Maya
A Mother's Story by Eleanor Vincent
"Vincent's poignant decision to donate Maya's organs will resonate with even hard-boiled readers." *Booklist*

Leaving the Hall Light On
A Mother's Memoir of Living with Her Son's Bipolar Disorder and Surviving His Suicide by Madeline Sharples
"A moving read of tragedy, trying to prevent it, and coping with life after." *Midwest Book Review*

Everything I Never Wanted to Be
A Memoir of Alcoholism and Addiction, Faith and Family, Hope and Humor by Dina Kucera
"Raw and funny." Joel Stein, *Time Magazine* columnist

Daughters of Absence
Transforming a Legacy of Loss, ed. by Mindy Weisel
"Essays by daughters of Holocaust survivors whose work has been both a life force and a lifesaver." *Booklist*

Be There Now
Travel Stories from Around the World,
ed. by Julie Rand and Mike O'Mary
"Travel pieces that capture the exterior world and offer a vivid sense of personal reflection." *Brevity*

Saying Goodbye
To the People, Places and Things in Our Lives,
ed. by Julie Rember and Mike O'Mary
"If you have ever had to deal with loss, read this book." *Midwest Book Review*

MFA in a Box
A Why to Write Book by John Rember
Winner of Hoffer, Nautilus and Midwest Book Awards. "The essential truths about excellent writing." The Hoffer Awards

Wise Men and Other Stories
Lessons From the Holidays by Mike O'Mary
Essays in the tradition of Robert Fulghum, Dave Barry, Bill Bryson, and other great American humorists.

Made in the USA
Lexington, KY
02 August 2016